HOW
TO MAKE IT
WHEN YOU'RE
CASH POOR
Revised and Updated

Hollis Norton

A Fireside Book
Published by Simon & Schuster, Inc.
NEW YORK

Copyright © 1985, 1986 by Hollis Norton
All rights reserved
including the right of reproduction
in whole or in part in any form
First Fireside Edition, 1986
Published by Simon & Schuster, Inc.
Simon & Schuster Building
Rockefeller Center
1230 Avenue of the Americas
New York, New York 10020
FIRESIDE and colophon
are registered trademarks of Simon & Schuster, Inc.
Designed by Barbara Marks
Manufactured in the United States of America
5 7 9 10 8 6   Pbk.
Library of Congress Cataloging-in-Publication Data
Norton, Hollis.
How to Make it when you're cash poor.
"A Fireside book."
Bibliography: p.
Includes index.
1. Real estate investment. 2. Success in business. I. Title.
HD1382.5.N67 1986   332.63′24   86-26174
ISBN 0-671-62803-8 Pbk.

TO THE HUNDREDS OF THOUSANDS OF
REAL ESTATE INVESTORS TO WHOM
I'VE SPOKEN, AND WHOSE IDEAS,
QUESTIONS, DOUBTS AND TRIUMPHS
HAVE HELPED MAKE THIS BOOK POS-
SIBLE.

Contents

Introduction

There are four things you need to know about Hollis Norton:

First and probably foremost, he's a self-made millionaire by following the program he outlined in this book. This country has become overpopulated with hundreds of thousands of so-called financial advisers and consultants who dispense dubious financial advice from their ivory towers. Happily for you, Hollis Norton is one of those rare exceptions—a man who has actually proven his ideas in the only laboratory that really counts—the marketplace.

Second, Mr. Norton is without a doubt the finest and most experienced real-estate lecturer in the country. In the past ten years he has spoken face to face with literally hundreds of thousands of real-estate investors. How does this relate to you? As a result of this vast teaching experience, he has heard every question, objection and doubt, and has learned how to cut through the fears of the average real-estate investor and motivate him to action. In short, he knows his stuff and knows how to teach it effectively. No one does it better.

Third, he can also write. The book you are about to read is excellent, and can really help you. It belongs in the library of every serious real-estate investor.

And finally, Hollis is one of my dearest and wisest friends. Wisdom is a rare prize. He possesses more than his share. I have drunk at his well often and always come away renewed. I encourage you to read on. You are in for a special feast.

—ROBERT ALLEN

1

WHAT ARE YOU WAITING FOR?

WE ALL KNOW THE AMERICAN DREAM. IT'S THE OLD, old dream that we can start with nothing, build it up to a fortune and be our own boss. We become free to work when we want, play when we want.

Lately the dream hasn't looked as real to some Americans as it used to.

How about you? Are you wondering whether you can survive these turbulent 1980s? Do you feel this terrible skidding feeling as you hear that the banks are about to go down the tubes, that you better keep a bag of silver under your bed because the butcher may accept a few coins when checks and credit cards and paper money are worthless, that the smart people are stocking their basements with canned food and preparing to defend it?

Not me. All this Noah's Ark talk doesn't bother me any more. I've heard it for too many years now. Meanwhile, I've proven to myself that the old-fashioned American dream is actually much closer to the truth than the nightmares about wheelbarrows full of thousand-dollar bills.

I say anyone can be wealthy. Sounds trite, doesn't it? And yet I'm totally convinced of it. I believe I could take any average working man and woman, spend a short period of time with them and, if they would listen (I mean really listen), show them how they could be financially independent in five years or less.

How I Learned

Five years is all it took me. When I was thirty-three years old I was purged out of the aerospace business along with umpty-nine others. I worked at many jobs, trying to eat and keep a roof over my head. My wife and I woke up one day, took a look down the road and didn't see how we were going to make it. We were getting nowhere financially. Working for someone else was no way to make the American dream come true.

So I decided to work for myself. I started experimenting with ideas. But with every good idea I hit on, the same roadblock popped up: money. I didn't have the money to get my idea past square one.

Finally a wealthy friend showed me a few simple ways to use other people's money—and make it grow for them as well as for me. It was no lazy man's way to wealth. It took study and work, but the methods succeeded almost automatically whenever I used them. The key was patience, keeping an eye on long-term growth and steady cash flow.

The Joy of Debt

There's no magic, no mystery about what I did. The steps were simple and clear-cut. This book blueprints them for you. Some of them seemed almost too good to be legal, but they really are legal—and ethical. I found out I had great credit because I owed a lot of money. There's nothing wrong with owing money if you borrow it for the specific purpose of making money with it, and if you know exactly how you're going to pay it back.

I just kept using borrowed money to build wealth for myself. Pretty soon it was bringing me a nice income—and has ever since.

I was asked to give lectures about it, and I enjoyed this almost as much as investing. Maybe more. I felt like the pro football player who retires to devote his time to coaching. I have always enjoyed sharing knowledge and helping people improve their financial position.

Could This Be You?

In the past eight years I have lectured in person to more than half a million people all over the United States. I've seen an exciting thing happen many times. It's especially noticeable in the question-and-answer period after my lectures. A widening of the eyes, a certain tilt of a head when someone starts to understand—the moment when the realization hits: "This guy is talking about me!"

I retired twice and after a while found myself almost throwing up on the golf course. I found I couldn't just play golf for the next fifty years (if I live that long). Desert islands don't relax me for more than a week. I found out I need people. I like touching lives.

That's why I'm writing this book.

I really would like to touch your life—if you want to commit yourself to doing what I tell you to do. Everything you're about to learn in this book has been tested, tried and proven by thousands of persons. So it can work for you too.

Financial Superstitions

You have nothing to lose except some "common sense" beliefs that are closer to superstitions, such as:

"The rich get all the good investment opportunities."

"You need ready cash to make money."

"What goes up must come down."

"Don't invest when times are uncertain."

"Pay as you go."

"Win through intimidation."

"Nice guys finish last."

To build wealth you must learn to think and do things differently. Quit following old paths blindly because the herd follows them. Ask questions. When people tell you "That's how it's always been done," I want you to say "Why?"

Let me tell you a story that illustrates the point.

Mystery of a Ham

A lady helping to prepare a meal noticed that her friend cut off both ends of a ham before placing it in the pan. She asked, "Why did you do that?" Her friend thought for a moment and replied, "I don't know. My mother always did it."

Out of curiosity, they decided to call her mother and ask her why. The mother said, "I don't know. My mother always did it."

Now they were really curious. They called the grandmother, who said, "I used to, but I don't any more." They asked, "Why not?" She replied, "Well, they're making the pans larger now."

I'll bet you do a lot of things without knowing why.

I want to shake you out of your rut so you can experience financial freedom. As you read this book, your mind will start to turn away from the nine-to-five treadmill and the after-dinner TV and turn toward endeavors that produce wealth. Then, as you build wealth, a light bulb will flash in your head and you'll exclaim, "Hey, this was here all along!"

In Case of Collapse

Everything that has happened to me financially in the past ten years could have happened in my early twenties. The principles worked then, and will always work. Now that I know what I know about success, if our whole system collapsed and another Great Depression came and I lost absolutely everything, I could have it back in just a few short years. Once you understand how wealth is created, you never lose your capacity to create it.

Safety is not in material things. You can lose all those. Safety is between your ears—your mind. You'll always possess the basic techniques for amassing wealth, once you've learned them. So knowledge becomes your real safety. Still, all the knowledge in the world is useless without action.

Your real enemy is inertia. Whether or not you get out of your rut depends on how badly you want something. If your desire for happiness and financial freedom is strong enough, you'll stop making excuses and get to work.

When I lecture to people about making money, I can always pick out the ones who think there's a way to wealth without work. When I mention work, some people get fidgety, nudge each other and look for an exit.

How much work am I talking about?

Five to ten hours of your spare time every week.

Sure, it sounds like a lot. But if you work smart, the time you invest will eventually be compensated at a rate of several hundred dollars per hour.

Maybe you're thinking, "I'm too busy. I won't have time."

Well, that's up to you. But I know this: We all find time for the things we really want to do. It's just a matter of priorities.

Who Cares?

Think it over. If one fact of life hasn't occurred to you before, let me make you aware of it now. Nobody cares about you financially—except you. If I'm in Hawaii next month playing golf and you're not there because you can't afford it, I'm not going to miss you—any more than you would miss me if you were there and I wasn't.

If you're lucky, the organization you work for will

keep you on the payroll for thirty years or so. If you're unlucky, you may be out on the street much sooner (as I was). Sooner or later you're going to be rewarded for your faithful service by being thrown out in the street. Who cares? Nobody. Except you.

The only way to make sure your income will continue into old age is to get off your *ass*ets and use your spare time to build some real wealth. That's what this book is all about.

You've got to care enough to commit some spare time. And maybe a little money if you have it. (If you don't have money to spare, these methods are even more important.)

Ready? Go!

Let's get started. To begin with, here are four simple suggestions that helped me when I was starting.

1. Buy a diary. A simple, cheap one is fine. Write down some financial goals and record your progress toward achieving them. Goals—I bet you don't have any. In my lectures I ask, "How many people have written financial goals?" Only three or four hands go up in an audience of four or five hundred people.

But when I ask, "How many people have written wills?" hundreds of hands go up. People plan more for their death than for their life! Isn't that interesting?

You'll also need your diary to keep a record of how much time you spend working toward your goals. By logging the hours spent, you'll be seeing whether or not you're living up to the mental commitment you made. It's a way of nudging yourself.

Stop Wasting Time

2. Quit watching television. If the TV habit is strong, the only way to kick it is suddenly—cold turkey. Get

tough with yourself. Take the TV plug out of the wall socket and cut off the plug with scissors.

That's the time to make up your mind about the financial goals I mentioned a minute ago. Write in the diary, "I can have the TV back when I have accomplished ————." You fill it in. You'll be surprised (especially during your favorite sports playoffs) how rapidly you'll go out and get the work done.

3. Plan a reward. A bigger reward, I mean, than plugging in the TV again. Pick something you've always wanted to do. A cruise on an ocean liner. A trip to a dream place. Reward yourself when your net worth is $200,000, maybe, or whatever major goal you've set. While you're out putting in the hours and building your wealth, you can dream a little about your reward. It can spur you on when your enthusiasm lags.

Stop Wasting Money

4. Don't buy things that depreciate in value. Of course you have to have a few, like appliances. But stop buying large things that go down in value. For example:

Boats. Don't buy one. Rent or lease for the time you'll be using it. A boat can go down in value thousands of dollars very quickly, but you'll be amazed how little it costs to rent one. (When you're wealthy, you can rent a yacht.)

Recreational vehicles. Again rent, don't buy. Use one on your vacation and turn it back in. I've heard all about how much you save on hotel bills. Well, when was the last year you spent thousands of dollars in hotels? (A recreational vehicle can go down that much in value in a single year.)

Cars. I know you need a car. But you don't have to buy it new and take a big loss later. Call up your local banks and ask to talk to the person in charge of repossessions (repos). Tell them you want a car and ask them

what they have. The list will startle you. They will name
a selling price, but you can make an offer below it. Also,
in many cases, you can buy for little or no money down
with the bank carrying the loan.

If you're going to build wealth, you're going to have
to throw away a set of keys. I call them the four keys to
failure. They were given to you by some well-meaning
people: parents, teachers, friends. They are:

1. Get a job, work all your life and get the gold watch
from a grateful company.

2. Save your money for a wonderful retirement.

3. Pay your taxes—it's a patriotic thing to do.

4. If you want to invest, dabble in the stock market.

Does all of that work? Take a look at the old people
in this country. They did it. They're also dead broke.
They don't have two nickels to rub together. They're a
national disgrace. If you're doing the above four things,
if that's your battle plan, you don't have a prayer of
making it financially. For your life to change you have to
change your habits. Now, let me show you what to do.

2

HOW TO EAT
A COW

How do you eat a cow? Simple. One steak at a time.

If I led you to a cow and suggested, "Eat it," you might wonder what kind of lunatic I was. If I offered to cook the cow for you, you might be polite enough to explain why you weren't that hungry and never could be.

And yet, if I offered you a small steak every few days and suggested, "Eat it," you'd probably do so. After a while you would have eaten the whole cow. Most of us eat many cows over a lifetime.

This is just another way of stating a principle that wise men have kept pointing out through the ages. An Oriental proverb says that a long journey begins with a single step. Thomas Babington Macaulay said, "Knowledge advances by steps, not by leaps." The Nobel Prize-winning scientist Pavlov told the youth of Russia, "From the very beginning of your work, school yourself to gradualness in the accumulation of knowledge."

How to Learn Real Estate Investing

If I point out a piece of real estate and say, "Buy it," to a person who has never bought real estate, the reaction would be about the same as if I'd suggested eating a cow. Seen from outside, the field of real-estate investing looks too vast and complex to enter.

21

Sure, it *is* vast and complex. The sheer number of wealth-building techniques to be found in real estate makes outsiders afraid of trying to figure out which techniques are best in their own personal situations—and also afraid of making the wrong choices.

Plain old human inertia is involved, too. It's hard to push ourselves into doing something different. That's another reason why most people pass up opportunities.

If only they could realize how easy it is to start investing in real estate.

If only they could realize how little capital they need.

If only they could realize that it's quite possible for them to retire with actual wealth—not just enough to get by.

Once they realized these truths, they would overcome fear and inertia. They'd start "eating the cow." I hope that's what you'll do, because I'm going to take the buying of real estate and break it down into small understandable parts.

My figure of speech about cow-eating doesn't assume that you'll eat the entire cow, hoofs, hide and all—only the meaty parts. Likewise, when I say you'll learn real-estate investing one part at a time, I don't mean that I'll teach you all its vastness and complexity. I'll just serve you what you need and can digest.

What We'll Skip

For instance, I won't teach you how to buy foreclosed properties, even though big profits can be made that way. That kind of investing calls for more experience and shrewdness and sheer predatory instinct than you'll ever get from a book. When you bid at a trustee sale, sheriff sale or others like it, you'd better know exactly what you're doing, because there are animals down there, and they eat amateurs. Four bidders can be working together, and you'll never know it. They will bid a house up, and then drop it on you. After you've left, they will divide up the rest of the properties.

Another big part I won't go into is the strategy of buying small fixer-uppers and pyramiding them. Many courses teach this. If you like paint and hammers and nails and stuff like that, there are great courses to take. Fixer-uppers are great money-makers. They are also complex and time-consuming. I think it's easier for the average person to buy good real estate with only a little cash, and hold it, than it is to go out and get involved with buy-and-upgrade operations. This book is for people who'd rather make money with their minds than with their hands.

I'll give you only one chapter on managing an apartment building or a string of houses. Whole books have been written on managing these. Being an owner-manager may bring you a good income if you do it right, but there are far easier ways to get a good income in real estate. If you want to make ten dollars an hour, go out and paint your apartments. If you want to make two hundred dollars an hour, go out and write offers. The buying process itself is where the wealth is made, not in the mundane work of managing, fixing up, etc. Still, in case you do find yourself in a spot where you can't afford to pay for even part-time management of your property, I'm including a short, simple survival guide for managers.

Don't Gobble

In this book you'll find all the techniques you need if you don't have much cash to invest or much leisure time. When you've finished the book you should be able to make yourself financially independent for the rest of your life. Understanding it, you'll gain confidence and lose your fear of buying.

However, I hope you won't devour the book at one

reading and put it away. Like steaks, these chapters are meant to be eaten slowly and chewed well. They're in logical order, so that the later ones build on the early ones. And you can use some of the early chapters before you even read the later ones.

I start by defining your investment. Real estate includes many different kinds of investment property: single-family homes, apartments, vacant lots, commercial buildings, industrial structures and so on. First you need to decide which of these will be most comfortable for you as an investor. I've laid out the pros and cons to help you understand them.

After you've read Chapter 4 and thought about it awhile, you can make a choice and start looking at properties. Then it's time to read Chapter 5, where you'll learn ways to narrow down your looking. You don't want to rush around helter-skelter. I'll help you understand what (and who) you're looking for, and where to look.

Making Your Reading Time Count

I'm guessing that most of you who read this book are now working at a full-time job. If so, five or ten hours a week are probably the most you can spare for your investment program right now. One way to make every hour count is to zero in on investments requiring little down payment.

I'll show you how to find them quickly in places investors seldom look—such as the lease-option ads in your daily newspaper, and the "for rent" ads. These are beautiful sources for the kind of investment I recommend. I'll take you through the newspaper itself, teach you how to read the ads.

When you've digested Chapter 5 and browsed in the ads awhile, maybe you'll be ready to go talk to a few of the advertisers. At that point, read Chapter 6. It tells you what to say to a seller when you call him up. You'll learn the right words to come out of your mouth. If you don't learn that, you're going to pay heavy freight out there, and you may never even know you've lost the money.

The Down-Payment Problem

The standard way to buy real estate is to pay 25 percent down, with conventional financing (probably a 25-year amortized loan at steep interest from a bank or savings and loan). That's the roughest way in the world to buy real estate. The underlying purpose of my whole book is to help you get away from that. Often you can reduce a down payment that someone says can't be cut.

It's possible to buy property with a down payment, yet not put down any cash of your own. I've included a chapter on alternative forms of down payment. Many of you have an acceptable down payment sitting in your garage or basement or backyard, or other places you haven't thought about. You'll be amazed to learn what some people will accept for a down payment.

And, of course, cash is all right for a down payment, if it isn't *your* cash. In Chapter 8 you'll find twenty-two ways to buy property when you're cash poor. Still more of these are in Chapters 14, 15, and 16. Study them one or two at a time.

Most of these ways involve borrowing from someone —using credit, in other words. A few of you may be worried about credit problems. Maybe you have a poor credit rating, or no credit at all? For your benefit I've included quite a bit of material on ways to buy real estate with no credit (I've used them myself) and ways to establish credit very quickly.

Make Me an Offer

Certain types of owners will be open to the financing ideas you'll learn in this book, but they won't suggest such ideas themselves. It's up to you to spell out an idea in writing, then make written adjustments in the course of negotiation. I know some of you are thinking that brokers will do that for you. Never let a broker write your offer. The broker represents only the seller. That's what the listing contract says. You're the buyer, and the more you pay, the bigger the broker's commission. So you must structure your own offers, and you need a basic understanding of how to do this. You'll find one whole chapter on it, plus tips throughout the book.

What happens when your offer is accepted? Then there'll be a "closing," as it's called, when a handful of documents will be passed around the table for everyone to sign. It's nice to be comfortable with the documents and the closing itself. Spotting clauses that work against you, and negotiating them out, can make all the difference in the world. I'll give you pointers about what to look for. But you'll need help.

Experts Who Can Help You

There's no requirement that you plunge into real-estate investing naked and alone. In fact, you shouldn't. If you have to ask how to play poker after you're at the table, better not play.

You can gather your own little circle of advisers with special knowledge and expertise. Try to line up an attorney and a CPA before you start, if you can afford them. And look around for other people who can advise you from time to time—people who know real estate and the neighborhood.

Let's start with an attorney. Many lawyers are fog lovers and nit-pickers by nature. Try to find one who'll talk straight and get to the point fast. Lawyers who are smart and well trained can tell you when to sign or not sign contracts and agreements. They can draft ironclad agreements for you to have other people sign. They can advise you on risks and remedies. Sometimes they can get bureaucrats and complainers off your back.

Recently I saw an article in *Success* magazine which insisted, "We're a nation of hustlers and confidence men." It seemed to imply that you should take advantage of others before they take advantage of you. I don't believe this. Other parties to a transaction needn't be your adversaries. You can structure an agreement so everyone benefits. Still, defensive real estate is sometimes important. You should know how to defend yourself when you walk into a broker's office or into an owner's home. I'll give you the main ideas to keep in mind.

But after a transaction is agreed on, if you run into problems about performance, and the other party is represented by a lawyer, it's nice to have your own lawyer step in. Then the discussion is on a lawyer-to-lawyer level. Lawyers understand each other. They can work out settlements for their clients' benefit without the hassle that laymen might get into.

Choosing a Lawyer

Most of the books and seminars advise you to choose a lawyer by asking around. I don't think this works very well, because people recommend their friends, their relatives, their own lawyers. None of these may be right for your particular needs.

Instead, go to your public library and look at a copy of the Martindale-Hubbel Law Directory, which lists lawyers' backgrounds and types of practice. If you have a contract question (say, about a bank-loan agreement) you want a contract specialist. If it's a real-estate matter, you want a real-estate attorney. The directory will show which firms in your area might help. Pick a few and ask some friendly real-estate people about them.

However, don't pick a firm with forty-seven attorneys, seven of whom have run for governor or hope to.

If a big law firm does take you on as a client, your work will be done by clerks in the back offices. And don't hire a young lawyer who has just opened his office. You need someone young but not too young—someone with enough experience to have a few scars, and enough energy to work hard for small clients. Generally you'll find him in a small firm or in private practice.

One more warning. Don't let your lawyer handle the financial provisions of a lease or an option. Even with good real-estate knowledge, he may not understand intricate cost calculations such as escalation clauses. And he's seldom familiar with local market conditions. So when it comes to the numbers in your documents, be guided by a good CPA. Or bring in a real-estate broker as a consultant for a particular transaction. Offer him a fee based on hours worked, whether the sale closes or not.

Choosing an Accountant

A good Certified Public Accountant (CPA) is worth his or her weight in rubies. Unless you are really low on cash and absolutely can't afford it, get a good one. In the long run, good accountants cost nothing, because they save you more in tax dollars than they charge you in fees.

Again, you want a CPA who is oriented toward real-estate investing. The firm must think in terms of maximizing your deductions and minimizing your income tax. The problem with most CPAs and other accountants is that they are too timid. They discourage deductions. I remember meeting the CPA of a good friend of mine, and his motto in preparing tax returns seemed to be "You cared enough to pay the very most."

Another one said to me, "Why not go ahead and pay the tax? Otherwise it's too much trouble." One reason for this attitude: Since 1980 the government has begun pressuring accountants to treat clients much as an IRS auditor would. It has been nicking them with "negligence penalty" fines of one hundred dollars per return for over-looking small technical errors, even when the client is mainly to blame. I think maybe the IRS hopes to scare them into "red-flagging" every questionable item on a return—that is, calling it to auditor's attention. The good CPAs are resisting this, but you have to pay more for their time.

Your best source of tax help may be the biggest ac-counting firm near you. Even if you are a small investor just starting out, most of these firms have real-estate spe-cialists who'll help you. But chat with them first, to get an idea of their willingness to argue with the IRS.

Other good bets would be to inquire in your local Apartment Owners' Association, or talk to a friend who is a successful real-estate investor. Ask: "Who does your taxes? What do you think of him?" The search is worth-while. When you find a good CPA he'll encourage you on your path, not give you reasons why it can't be done.

Others Who Can Help You

If you have a little money to trade for time, there are other ways to get useful advice. Talk to local real-estate brokers. Tell them you'd like to buy some investment property and ask what areas they would suggest. Ask about properties in good, middle- to upper-middle-class neighborhoods. Hearing the same names favorably sev-eral times turns these names into recommendations.

Another source of good ideas is a Certified Property Manager (CPM). These firms rent and manage apartment buildings in your area, so they have first-hand knowledge about the pros and cons of some neighborhoods you may be considering.

To find some of these firms, what some people do is to go into a neighborhood and look for signs that say something like "Managed by Jay Smith Associates."

Then they call up Jay, and tell him they hope to be buying a large number of units in the area and would like to talk to him about being a manager. He'll understand that before hiring him people want to make sure he is knowledgeable, so he'll be glad to answer questions like these:

"What's your average vacancy factor?"

"How hard are apartments to rent?"

"How do tenants feel about the neighborhood?"

And so on. A firm that wants to be hired will want to impress you with its knowledge.

Use your DBA (Doing Business As) card (explained in Chapter 5) when you talk to brokers and CPMs. The words "Property Acquisition" will make them pay attention to you. Also, wear the more expensive items in your wardrobe.

This book includes chapters on various special areas that small real-estate investors need to understand—such as income taxes (how not to pay them), rent control (how to cope with it), rate of return (a formula that shows how your investments are really doing) and balloon payments (what to do when they come due). All the methods described have been proven in practice.

Remember, when you divide a cow into steaks, it's easy to eat. Know-how and understanding can make you unafraid of investing. So go ahead and get started. I don't want to be your guru for the rest of your life. I want to make you independent of me so you won't need me anymore.

3

WHAT YOU NEED TO KNOW ABOUT REAL-ESTATE INVESTING

*"Ninety per cent of all millionaires be-
came so through owning real estate. More
money has been made in real estate than
in all industrial investments combined."*
— Andrew Carnegie

NOTICE THAT CARNEGIE, THE CANNY OLD SCOT, SAID "owning" real estate. Not "buying real estate and selling it."

There are many ways to make money in real estate. Carnegie used the one I'm going to teach you.

So did Marshall Field. Field built, owned and operated famous and successful department stores in Chicago, but he never said department stores were a good route to financial success. He said, "Buying real estate is not only the best way, the quickest way, and the safest way, but the *only* way to become wealthy."

He had to quit school at sixteen. He worked as a shop clerk, bought real estate and held it. The cash flow from his real estate gave him money to buy a partnership in a wholesale dry-goods company and eventually to start a department store. When the great Chicago fire of 1871 and the financial panic of 1873 threatened to wipe out his stores, he didn't have to go to banks and beg for loans. He just drew more income from his real-estate equities.

Each year *Forbes,* the financial magazine, makes a shrewd guess at who the 400 wealthiest Americans are. Of the 400 in the latest survey, 63 made their fortunes in real estate. Many of the others used real estate to build

31

up and preserve the capital they'd accumulated elsewhere (or inherited).

Still the Best Investment

Maybe you're thinking, "Sure, Carnegie and Field
and some of those others started small and built up
wealth in real estate. But that was long ago. What about
this year? I hear the real-estate market isn't so hot lately.
Inflation seems to have eased off. Can I still make it in
real estate?"

Yes. You definitely can—even if inflation stops dead,
even if real-estate prices level off. (For details about
what would happen to your wealth-building in that case,
see Chapter 14.)

Real estate is still the only vehicle that is going to take
a few hundred or a few thousand dollars of your money
and turn it into half a million in as little as five years, with
a high degree of safety. Other enterprises *may* do this—
sometimes—but they aren't safe. They are speculations.
Real estate stays useful and valuable regardless of the
economic cycle. Its profits are consistent in the long run,
due to the simple laws of supply and demand.

As I said, there are many ways to make money in real
estate. Some people do it by picking up run-down properties, renovating them and selling at a profit. Some do it
by sniffing out bargains and turning them over fast. Some
do it by simply buying good property and selling when
the passing of time has fattened up the market value.
Some do it as builders and developers.

But the best way, I've always found, is to buy reasonably good income property and hold it, letting the rental
income make you independent. The system works best
and fastest if little or none of your own money is involved.

Again, you may be thinking doubtful thoughts: "He
makes it sound too easy. How can I buy property with
little or none of my own money?"

Debt Is Not a Four-Letter Word

You do it by borrowing. This is much easier than you think. You'll learn many easy ways to borrow in future chapters.

The old idea used to be, "Save your money. Savings can get you through the hard times." This no longer makes sense.

The more you learn about investment, the more you'll realize that the key to making real estate pay is borrowing. At first you may be horrified at the thought of owing tens of thousands of dollars. But keep on reading this book, and start some small experimenting when you're ready. Soon you won't be bothered at all by owing hundreds of thousands, or even millions, because you'll have more than enough monthly income to pay the monthly interest charges.

In real estate, borrowing is called leverage. Leverage is making a little money earn a lot. Look at the arithmetic. Let's say somebody has $50,000 of his own money, and he wants to buy a $100,000 property. He doesn't understand leverage. So, using the old thinking, he puts all his cash down, and takes a $50,000 mortgage for the rest of the purchase price. Now let's imagine he sells the property a year later for a startling price, $150,000, and pays off the mortgage. Hurrah, he's $50,000 ahead, and he's doubled his money, if we ignore the minor costs along the way. Sounds good, doesn't it?

But wait. What if he'd used more leverage? Suppose his down payment was only $10,000 instead of $50,000. Then he would almost quintuple his investment. And he could have put the other $40,000 into other properties. At that same rate of return, he could have invested his $50,000 and come out with about $250,000.

Why is borrowing easy in real estate? Because the lender's money is secured by visible, touchable, usable property that won't run away. If the borrower doesn't pay, the lender just takes back the property.

And this kind of debt makes sense for the borrower because real estate earns more than it costs the borrower in interest (or "debt service," as money men call it).

You'll never get into trouble if you make sure that income from the property, plus the tax savings that ownership gives you, will cover the debt service. In other words, budget your use of credit as you would your use of cash.

Debt Is Transformed into Wealth

This may sound crazy at first—but every dollar in real-estate debt today is a dollar in net worth in eight or ten years.

What you want to be worth a few years from now, you have to owe today. If you'd like half a million, go out and buy property until you control half a million in mortgage debt. Then just wait. Time will take care of the rest. The property will double in value, and every dollar in debt becomes a dollar in equity.

Years ago, I began showing people how to pick up parcels of apartment real estate for low down payments and easy terms. An average building might have six tenants; each tenant may be paying $125 per month at that time. Today these renters probably pay $250 or $300. These are long-term, low-income tenants who want this sort of housing, are glad to rent it, and stay in it. Some of them stay thirty years. Just one thirty-year resident might pay a total of $30,000 or $40,000 during his occupancy—more than the owner's total original investment in the building. In addition, the total paid to the owner by the five other tenants may now be $20,000 to $30,000 per year, all pure profit since he got rid of the mortgage. You might pick up a half-dozen such low-rent multiple dwellings for small first investments—and that's just one way to invest.

Some older people still think the best way to buy

anything, including real estate, is with all cash, because then you don't have to pay interest. This doesn't make much sense today. It means you can't buy nearly as much as you would otherwise.

Even if the inflation rate is only 5 percent a year (and it's much higher most years) a buyer will need $105,000 next year to buy things that cost $100,000 this year. If he doesn't use leverage, his financial progress will be almost nil. The only times you should pay all cash (for real estate and most other things that go up in value) is when cash will get you a big discount. I'll go into more detail about that later in the book.

Two Problems Solved

Anyhow, we're assuming that you're cash poor. So you face two problems as a real-estate investor:

1. Even if you would prefer to, you can't make the large down payment that is the conventional way of buying real estate.

2. You need to build wealth faster than investors who start with plenty of capital.

Both problems are solved at once when you buy real estate with little or no down payment. The less you put down, the bigger your return on each dollar you invest. This allows you to build wealth quickly.

Figure the return on your invested dollar in terms of percentage, like the interest yield on your bank savings or your stocks and bonds. This return is the increase in value of your real estate divided by your down payment. Let's look at some examples to see how different the return can be for investors making different down payments on the same property.

What Percentage Does Your Investment Yield?

We'll say a property cost $100,000 and is worth $110,000 a year later. First consider the all-cash buyer I mentioned a moment ago. He paid $100,000. So he got a 10 percent return on his money. A generation ago, 10 percent was pretty good. But today he might get better than 10 percent on a bank certificate of deposit, or a utility bond.

Now consider the fellow I mentioned a few pages before. He bought a $100,000 property with a $50,000 down payment. If the property appreciates $10,000 in a year, his return is 20 percent ($10,000 is ⅕ of $50,000, or 20%).

Figure the same increase in value but only a $20,000 down payment, and the equation is

$$\frac{\$10,000 \text{ increase}}{\$20,000 \text{ down payment}} = \begin{array}{l} 50\% \text{ payback on the cash} \\ \text{invested.} \end{array}$$

What about a $10,000 down payment?

$$\frac{\$10,000 \text{ increase}}{\$10,000 \text{ down}} = 100\% \text{ return.}$$

Or, a $1,000 down payment?

$$\frac{\$10,000 \text{ increase}}{\$1,000 \text{ down}} = 1,000\% \text{ return.}$$

Now imagine how your return would go up if, on that same property and with the same 10 percent appreciation, your down payment was only $500 or $250. Or how about nothing down? On such percentages of return your net worth goes up pretty fast, doesn't it? What other safe investment can yield such profits?

Yes, it really is possible to put down only a few hundred dollars, or nothing, and become owner of a property that will increase in value by 10 percent (or considerably more) per year over the course of a few years.

You can't negotiate such a transaction with every seller, I admit. But there are a surprising number who'll do it. I'll show you how to find them in Chapter 5 and how to negotiate with them in Chapter 6.

Again you may be wondering: "That's all well and good, but how about the monthly payments?"

The conventional thinking is, "If the down payment is smaller, the monthly payment has to be bigger." But this thinking is often wrong.

In real estate, terms are as important as price (or often *more* important). Get this concept firmly in mind before you buy or sell. What it means is that the lower price isn't necessarily best for the buyer. Nor is the highest price necessarily best for the seller.

Down Payment and Monthly Interest Can Both Be Small

The cash-poor property hunter, if he knows how to hunt, can find sellers who are perfectly willing to accept more paper at a lower interest rate, and wait longer to get paid off, than the average seller is. Such flexible sellers make a bigger profit in the long run than they would otherwise. And you, as buyer, can show them this with pencil and paper.

I'm getting a bit ahead of myself, because I'll explain all this fully in Chapters 5 and 6, but let me say briefly what you do: You find a good property for sale by a seller who no longer wants to own the property, and isn't in urgent need of cash. It might be somebody who's being transferred, getting a divorce, retiring—whatever.

In order to make a quick sale, he's willing to be flexible on both your down payment and your installment payments. He'd just as soon receive small steady payments for a long time than be confronted with the problem of where to invest a big chunk of cash, or big installment payments.

This is the kind of seller who often takes paper instead of a down payment, so you may not have to produce any cash, or only a little. The most common paper is a second or third mortgage, which means that if you default, the lender would have only second or third claim on the money brought in by the foreclosure sale of the property. The first mortgage holder (usually a bank or a savings and loan) is first in line for whatever it lent on the property. However, the foreclosure sale should bring enough to pay all the mortgages. Most owners understand this and don't lend more on their property than it is worth.

Of course, I'll show you how to make sure you'll never have to default on your debt—in other words, how to structure your offer so the rental income (cash flow) will cover the mortgage payments and operating expenses, with a safety margin left over. Read all about this in Chapter 11.

So, to sum up, the central fact you need to understand about real-estate investment is the difference between constructive debt and destructive debt. The difference depends on what you do with the money you borrow. If you put it to work earning more than the carrying charges, it is constructive debt.

A mortgage is constructive debt. (So is a credit-card debt if you pay it promptly, with no late charges or interest. That's simply getting an interest-free loan for a month or so.)

Some other debts are constructive wealth-builders too, if they conserve your cash for uses that will bring in more profit than the cost of servicing the debt. Incurring debt for the specific purpose of netting a profit is standard practice in the business and investment worlds.

A destructive debt, if you're paying interest on it, is a debt for anything that is *decreasing* in value. If you run up finance charges for groceries or clothes or furniture or a car or a vacation trip, that's destructive. It wastes your capital. Your debt load makes you poorer, not richer.

Take on debt for real estate, and in a few years you can buy the finest car you want, without borrowing to do so. You'll be able to enjoy a fine home, foreign travel and the other comforts and luxuries of financial independence. My system of investing will do all this for you. Read on and see exactly how!

4

WHICH KIND OF REAL ESTATE FOR YOU?

YOU'VE READ THREE CHAPTERS AND YOU'RE STILL WITH me. That means you're probably going to make many real-estate investments during the rest of your life.

These could be land, houses, apartment or office buildings or storefront properties. Before you decide what kind of real estate to start with, I think it's important that you have a basic understanding of their good and bad points. (We won't even look at more exotic kinds such as farms, factory buildings, ranches and so on. These are much more businesses than real-estate investments.)

The Lure of Raw Land

Since it's the simplest form of realty investment, let's start by considering empty undeveloped land.

As a money maker it looks beautifully simple, doesn't it?

You just buy acreage in the country, or a vacant lot in a city or town, then forget it until the buyers come knocking at your door. The land can't deteriorate (except a flood or a landslide). It can't be burned or stolen. It isn't taxed heavily. You have no management worries, nothing to do except dream about the profits you'll make.

Easy money—or is it?

I know a lot of you own land. Maybe you bought

because you were convinced that land must keep rising in value. Isn't the supply limited? Isn't population growing and spreading out? "The United States is running out of land," some salesmen say.

Oh, those smooth salesmen! Phones and post offices are kept busy by high-pressure outfits peddling land for second homes, retirement homes, homesteading—and especially for investment. They'll treat you to a free roast-beef dinner and then hand you a contract to sign by candlelight. Should you look at the land first? "No need," the salesmen say, "because we represent a big, reliable company listed on the stock exchange."

They may tell you (and it's true) that in 1974 a Dallas real-estate group sold for $45,000 a patch of weedy soil that they bought only two months earlier for a mere $6,000. Or that in Honolulu, a few years ago, one empty four-and-a-half-acre parcel sold for $175,000, was resold a few days later for $250,000 and sold again two years later for a half million. Yes, Virginia, there is a Santa Claus, and yes, there are land booms sometimes.

And yes again, a small speculator can occasionally cash in on a boom before it busts. I know of a lawyer in New Jersey who bought Florida land for $253 an acre and sold to another trader for $322, who in turn sold for $472—all within one year. Four-fifths of this acreage was under water. Did they all know? Don't ask!

Beware of the Hot Deal

Land booms can be like the old chain-letter pyramids. Each buyer in turn plans to get out from under by selling to another greedy speculator. The last speculator, if he's lucky, sells to the ultimate buyer, the developer. The developer prices the costly land into his units, figuring he'll get his heavily leveraged money back by unloading on the public.

This used to work most of the time. But lately the

public is wising up, so overpriced tract homes are harder to sell. Some big subdividers have gone broke. Knowing this, many other developers now walk away from overpriced land, and parcels lie unsold, piling up tax bills. The last buyer can't get his money out.

Land sold by "land companies" is marked up four to five times over its current market value. If you don't believe me, price the land they *don't* own nearby.

And beware of potential fraud, because hidden problems can make rural land worthless for future development. For instance, electricity may not be close by, or the soil may not support septic tanks, or worst of all, there is no water.

Also, don't believe all you hear about the supply of land running short. New Jersey, our most urbanized state, is still three-fourths rural. Even without counting Alaska and Hawaii, almost nine-tenths of the total land area in the U.S. is virtually empty. Most farm towns are shrinking, not growing.

What about downtown land or vacant lots in residential areas? Don't buy unless you're sure a builder will want them. If you guess wrong, your money may be locked up in unsalable acreage for a long, long time.

Arithmetic of a Land Investment

Maybe you're thinking to yourself, "Yeah, but I know some good territory on the edge of a fast-growing city, and I bet I'll make a bundle if I buy and hold for five years or so. I can buy direct from an old lady who owns it."

Well, let me take you through an actual land investment. Let's say you and I go out there right now and buy a piece of land for $10,000. The price doesn't matter in the example, but $10,000 is a round number we can work with. We intend to sell after five years.

Let's try to maximize our profit. Pretend the old lady agrees to fantastic terms—no down payment, and only

$100 monthly installments. That's about the best anyone could hope for. Looks like we've got a luscious peach ripening on the tree. But wait, we have more figuring to do.

Interest on our loan? Say 8 percent, to complete the rosy view.

So now we sit back and watch our land go up in value —"appreciate," as the money men say.

How much will it appreciate? For our example, let's try 15 percent per year. The actual national average for land appreciation is only 3¼ percent—but we'll say this is good land and it will go up much faster.

Now let's see what the yearly 15 percent rise does for us in profit.

It means the land gains $1,500 in value every year, for a total of $7,500 in five years. So let's assume we'll sell for $17,500.

But it costs a little money to own land. Real-estate taxes come due every year—let's use a couple of hundred dollars for this example. We also have to pay something called "improvement assessments" for telephone lines and sewer bonds or other fees, if it's recreational land. If the land is close to town, we have to pay for things like weed abatement and trash pickups, because you can't have an eyesore near town. This costs us another couple of hundred.

And of course we have to pay interest on the $10,000 we borrowed. At 8 percent (a very conservative rate nowadays) that's $800 a year.

Altogether, then, our land is costing us maybe $1,200 a year in hard cash. After five years our total payout has been $6,000.

We started with a debt of $10,000, remember. Add our payout to this, and our land becomes a $16,000 investment. We sell for $17,500, leaving us a $1,500 profit —so far.

But selling land costs money. We have to pay a real-estate commission, which, by the way, is well earned.

Brokers and salesmen work hard to find buyers. Real-estate commissions on raw land can run as high as 10 percent on the sales price. Ten percent of $17,500 is $1,750 commission. But let's say we know the broker and he gives us a little break. We pay only $1,500.

Using those figures, we come out even. After five years there is no profit whatsoever.

An article in *U.S. News & World Report,* analyzing land transactions nationwide, stated that if your land isn't going up in value at least 20 percent each year, you're really sliding backward. Counting all the costs involved, 20 percent per year is a break-even point. Land seldom appreciates that fast.

In other words, investing in land without taking values into consideration can be a way of not making money for a long time.

There are three benefits of investing in real estate under the new 1986 tax law: cash flow from rentals, tax write-off for depreciation (assuming you meet income and management requirements of the new law—see Chapters 13 and 18), and buildup of equity as the loans are paid off (your percentage of ownership increases). You give up the first two of these benefits when you buy raw land. So my point is, you can't make money as a "passive" land investor—that is, by simply buying and holding.

There's one exception, though. If you're lucky enough to have advance knowledge of where an important development is going, and can buy in the path of that development, you can reap a bonanza. But for this kind of knowledge you need a brother-in-law who builds shopping centers and will tell you where they'll go up before anyone else knows. Or you need somebody who'll tip you off to the future location of the new municipal airport or military base or football stadium or some other major traffic builder. Just be sure the tip is true. Swindlers often plant false rumors to sell worthless land.

Bargains for Tax Sales

The amount of land you can buy is limited by the size of the payment you are able to make (based on your current salary or income). With that same money, or less, you can buy millions of dollars' worth of income property—because the tenants make the payments.

But this isn't to say you should positively never buy land. If you can pick up a real bargain, it may be worthwhile. Where are the bargains? At tax sales.

In this country a great deal of land is abandoned for various reasons. After the owners stop paying property tax, the state takes the land back for taxes and sells it off to recover the lost taxes. Plenty of land (especially raw land) can be bought for as little as 1/20th of its appraised value. Let's take an example:

An empty lot is appraised at $10,000. The owner wants to sell but there are no buyers. The owners get tired of holding it and paying property tax every year, so they let it go. You buy it at a tax sale for $2,000. Then you turn around and offer the land for a down payment for another property at the full value of $10,000 (you'll get some no's, but don't take them personally). You might add a cash sweetener if you have some more cash available. So—

$ 2,000 Cash
$10,000 Equity in Lot
$12,000 Down Payment

When you buy a property this way, you find yourself with $12,000 equity in it, even though you paid only $4,000 ($2,000 down payment plus $2,000 for the land). You'll find creative ways in this book to pull out that equity and put it to work.

If You Own Land, Develop It

As a land investor you should be active, not passive. Do something to increase your land's value. Of course this takes time, work and savvy.

Some examples:

1. Put a building on your lot. Then you can sell both land and building and make a profit on each.

2. Subdivide. That is, buy forty acres, break it down into small lots, double the price and resell. This is profitable if there are eager buyers, but you may have to pay a stiff tax on your gain.

3. Get your land's zoning upgraded to higher and better use by applying to your local planning commission. This automatically boosts its value to builders or developers; do what you can to enable you to charge a higher price per square foot.

The SFH: Money-Making, Fast-Appreciating, Many-Benefited

Let's move onto the second simplest kind of real estate, the single family home (SFH).

If I were a poet I'd write an ode to the SFH. Its benefits are almost too numerous to mention.

It's easy to buy one. Compared to other property, it's easier to borrow money on, easier to sell. There are great tax benefits. There's no worry about rent control. I could go on—but let's stop and look at these basic benefits.

There are always plenty of houses for sale by people who need to sell. The normal course of human events such as job changes, retirements, divorces and other happenstances create a never-ending stream of people whose need to sell is more urgent than their need for quick cash.

Almost any day you can find several new advertisements of houses for sale. This not only makes it easy to buy a house to live in, but almost always makes it easy for you to buy a series of SFHs to speed yourself toward your goal of financial freedom.

I've seen investors buy SFHs at the rate of one a week. Maybe you will, too, eventually. Just for a start, as soon as you know the principles, you should be able to go out into the marketplace and buy one or two per year. It's a reasonable goal.

Financing? No Problem

Even when money is tight and conventional lenders are saying no to almost everybody, there is money to lend for the SFH. Bankers and savings-and-loans officers consider it to be the safest investment to lend on. Another benefit: They lend on percentage of value. In most money markets you can get an 80 percent loan on a single-family home.

This isn't the case with apartments and office buildings. The maximum loan on them has dropped from 75 percent of appraised value down into the 50–60 percent range. That's because a conventional lender looks mainly toward their income, rather than their value, to support the loan.

Recently I inquired about refinancing a large office building I own. The new loan, lenders said, couldn't be for more than 57 percent of its appraised value (based on the current income).

Selling Is Easier

Investors are the only prospective buyers of "investment properties"—which means apartments and office buildings and the like. But there are two markets for SFHs. You can sell them either to investors or to families who want to live in them. Wherever there's a housing shortage, families who need homes will bid prices up

quickly and make you enormous profits. Severe shortages are predicted for the last half of the 1980s.

Office and apartment buildings don't increase in value
so fast. The price in any given area depends mainly on
the rents the property can command. As you gradually
raise rents over the years, you can raise your asking
price to buyers. In short, homes tend to appreciate faster
than income property—faster than any other real estate
—and are easier to sell.

But appreciation is only the frosting on the cake. Inflation could stop completely and property values might
stop rising, but those nice people who live in your property will still keep paying. Home renters are more stable
than apartment renters. They tend to stay a long time. (It
costs a lot to move all that furniture, kids will have to
change schools, etc.) Their rent will pay off that mortgage and buy the property for you. Then you'll own a
valuable asset to sell, trade or live in.

The main drawbacks to the SFH as an investment are
(1) fewer renters are available for homes than for apartments, yet you need more rent to handle your mortgage
payment; (2) if you have one vacancy you are 100 percent vacant—no cash coming in.

If you invest in an SFH, I'd like to see you buy in
middle-class or upper-middle neighborhoods—but buy
the cheaper housing in the better neighborhood. If prices
are from $50,000 to $80,000 in the neighborhood, buy the
$50,000 home, because if times get hard, the $50s will be
rented and the $80s won't.

Tax Breaks for the Investor

The 1986 Tax Reform Act has made significant
changes in real-estate tax law and should be addressed.
Capital gains were taken away. All sale profits are taxed
at the new ordinary income rates, either 15 percent or 28
percent (starting in 1988, the rate will depend on whether

your income is above or below $17,850 single or $29,750 married and filing jointly). The tax shelter (depreciation) has been removed as a source of offsetting salary for the passive investor. If you are involved in the management of the property, though, you can use depreciation to off-set income up to a maximum of $25,000. The key here is to be sure you are in compliance with the new law in order to qualify for the tax shelter. I strongly suggest you sit down with your CPA and real-estate tax attorney and work out a battle plan. You might, as an example, want to form a real estate management corporation (you being a major stockholder) and have that corporation contract with any management company that is running your properties. This $25,000 allowable tax shelter is phased out as your income exceeds $100,000 per year; however, not many of you reading this book should concern yourself with it. If you are blessed with this lovely problem, consult your tax advisor for details.

The depreciation schedules have been changed. Accelerated depreciation will end and be replaced with straight-line depreciation (an equal amount taken each year). For residential property you now use 27½ years, for all other property 31½ years. Let's take an example for a $100,000 rental house (except in a few areas, you can buy rentals cheaper than this). We can't depreciate land because the IRS won't let us. We'll assume the land is worth $20,000, so we're left with an $80,000 structure to depreciate. Remember, we now use 27½-year straight line, so you divide the $80,000 by 27.5 and get $2,909 per year. The $2,909 hasn't come out of your pocket, but you can claim it as a deduction on your income-tax return. This will save you $814 in income tax if you're in the 28 percent tax bracket and put an extra $68 in your pocket every month.

You don't have to wait until April 15 for income-tax relief. Estimate your tax savings after you close (or ask your tax man for help), reduce the withholding on your

paycheck, and enjoy the extra income immediately.
Want more tax savings? Buy two houses instead of one.
Buy three. Remember, you're entitled, as an owner involved in management, to $25,000 in deductions. Buy
enough property to take advantage of what the new law
gives you. Again, sit down with your tax advisor and
work out the details.

Rent Control? Not for the SFH

Rent control is already a fact of life in many cities.
We'll see more of it, not less, as vacancies get scarcer in
the years ahead. However, housing units of four or less
—including the SFH, naturally—are exempt from most
rent-control ordinances. This means you can raise your
SFH rents as much as the marketplace will allow, even
in a city under tight rent control.

Rent control always makes a housing shortage worse
—which should bring you more profit as an owner of
SFH rentals.

You Might Prefer Bigger Buildings

Because of the shortage of rental housing, veteran
investors favor apartment houses, followed by commercial buildings in cities where office space is scarce.

We'll get into more detail about the possibilities in
multi-unit properties in future chapters. For now, let's
just take a quick look at their good and bad points.

An important good point for investors: We're in the
worst housing crunch in about forty years. The government considers a 5 percent vacancy rate in a city to be a
housing shortage. The rate is under 2 percent in a lot of
cities. Los Angeles has only about 1 percent of its housing unoccupied; some people are living in autos and renting bathroom privileges from neighborhood tenements.

More important, the pent-up demand will probably
keep growing during the rest of the 1980s. Here's why.

Housing Wanted

The children born during the postwar baby boom have grown up now. More than 40 million people are reaching the age of thirty in this decade. Never before in our history have so many thirty-year-olds come along in one period.

Thirty is approximately the age when people form new households. Some experts estimate that about 1,830,000 new households will be formed each year through 1990. Even the most conservative put the rate at 1,300,000.

Too bad for those new families. Most of the 40 million-odd who'll try to buy their first home during this decade are going to find that the dream of owning a home is only a dream. They'll have to remain renters—mostly apartment renters. There just aren't enough houses for them. Few builders are putting up new houses because the costs are too high.

Of course, you don't necessarily have to start with a hole in the ground to add new units to the nation's housing supply. *The Wall Street Journal* reports that a fast-food drive-in in Atlanta, a grain elevator in Minneapolis and a church in New York have all been converted into dwelling units in recent years. Abandoned homes and tenements are being rehabilitated. Single-family homes are being turned into duplexes.

We'll see more and more such conversions as the crunch gets worse. Some cities may even become as crowded as Paris, where parents bequeath their rental apartments to their children.

If you're a landlord, you may eventually see two or three tenants bidding for your one vacant unit. You probably can't visualize $4,000 a month rent for an apartment any more than your grandfather, who paid $20 a month, could visualize $400 or $500. But if you live long enough you'll see $4,000 (salaries will be much higher due to inflation). What will a ten-unit building be worth when it takes in $40,000 a month in rents? Maybe you should pick up some ten-unit properties right now.

How Big Should You Start?

Everybody hears advice about buying real estate. What you probably hear most often is that the best way to start investing is to buy a two-flat or a four-flat which may cost only $100,000 or less.

Maybe that's right for you. Buy what you are comfortable buying. If you're comfortable with houses and I urge you to buy apartments, you probably aren't going to buy anything. You can make more money buying a house right than buying a ten-flat wrong. To buy right, of course, you need the right kind of seller. (We'll hear a lot more about that in the next chapter.)

Bear in mind, however, that the larger the property is, the less a single vacancy hurts your gross income. Moreover, it's easier to negotiate for a six- or eight-flat because there'll be fewer investors bidding against you. Most people are conditioned to think small, and there are always more buyers looking for two- or four-flats than there are sellers. For the amount of money they bring in rent, two- and four-family houses are much higher priced than sixes, and eights (because of higher demand). It's usually much easier to avoid negative cash flow if you buy six units and up.

What are the basic drawbacks to apartment investing? One is that you need good management. There's a higher turnover of tenants, which causes work for the manager in showing apartments and filling vacancies. And of course the manager must be ready to deal with all kinds of maintenance problems at all hours. He or she can't very well say, "I'll see about it Monday," if the plumbing shuts off Friday night.

Another drawback: As I mentioned earlier, the price

of an apartment building tends to rise more slowly than SFH prices. What an investor will pay depends mostly on how much rent the apartments pull in, and you can't raise apartment rents faster than the going rate in similar buildings. (Rent control, if it comes to your area, can be another big drawback—but I'll show you how to lick it, at least for the short term, in a later chapter.)

What About Shopping Centers and Business Buildings?

Commercial property is generally best suited to the big investor, because the drawbacks are discouraging to anyone starting small. Here they are:

1. Vacancies tend to be longer. Starting or moving a business (either in shop or office) is a much bigger decision than renting an apartment.

2. Recessions can produce a lot of vacancies—or can make it harder to collect rent from tenants. Many small businesses (and some big ones) go bankrupt.

3. Rent raises are slow. Therefore, the building's value goes up slowly.

4. If you buy shops in a badly designed development, you can be stuck with almost permanent vacancies. No merchant wants a shop where the traffic pattern sends people off in other directions.

Nevertheless, some investors prosper with shops and office properties, because of these advantages:

1. Successful businesses stay a long time.

2. Tenants don't damage property. It's to a businessman's advantage to have the property look great.

3. Because tenants are cooperative, commercial buildings are easy to manage.

What's Going to Happen?

It's really difficult to make predictions, and since you'll probably be reading this after the fact, you'll know. After having said that, here goes: I think loss of tax advantages will have a short-term adverse effect on the prices of apartment buildings and commercial properties (except perhaps for smaller owner-managed units) —perhaps as much as a 10 percent to 15 percent drop. Rents should increase sharply over the next few years (due to loss of tax benefits), which should bring prices back up. Single-family homes should not be affected a great deal, because the user-demand factor will still be strong. The interest deduction will still be available on first and second homes, and home ownership will be one of the last remaining tax shelters. I will be buying single-family homes until the middle to end of 1987. If there is a drop in prices for apartments during that time, we should look at it as a buying opportunity. The new laws should greatly slow down construction, which will help to escalate rents over the next few years and drive up the prices of apartment buildings. Except for a real steal, I would hesitate to buy commercial property over the next few years.

•   •

5

FINDING YOUR INVESTMENT

I'VE MET HUNDREDS OF PEOPLE WHO BUILT UP A QUARTER-million or a half-million dollars of net worth from virtually nothing. They did it in the marketplace, by buying real estate intelligently.

Now it's your turn. You don't need a genius IQ or a college education. You can start with a little money or you can start with no money. All you need, basically, is know-how (which you'll get from this book) and some time and energy.

You can keep your present job, if you have one. In five to ten hours a week of spare time, you can start building a second income in property—an income that in a few short years can actually be more than you're making now from full-time work on someone else's payroll.

Afraid of Real Estate?

Most people know that investing in real estate is about the surest and safest of all ways to make money. Yet most people won't try it.

Why? Fear. Fear paralyzes people, saps their energy.

Anyhow, fear is caused by lack of knowledge. We all tend to be afraid of what we don't understand. Countless people look at a good piece of property and say, "Well, it sure looks good but we don't understand real estate so we'd better not get involved." Or they say, "I'd like to buy, but I don't see how I can afford it." So they pass. And someone else picks up thousands of dollars in profit that could have been in their pockets.

Well, maybe you yourself are slightly scared at this moment. But you'll get over it as you keep reading. This book will give you the knowledge you need, thereby overcoming any fears and blocks you may feel at the thought of buying property.

Looking for Mr. Goodseller

Okay, let's get down to business. At the start, you will spend five or ten hours looking, and screening out properties that you shouldn't bother inquiring about. That's what we'll cover in this chapter. (In the next chapter I'll show you exactly how to approach the sellers who are worth approaching—and later I'll show you how to write offers.)

Right now you're just looking. But not for a property.

Instead, you're looking for a person. A certain kind of person. The kind who will sell his or her property without insisting on a big down payment or stiff monthly terms. In other words, someone whose need to sell is more pressing than his need for cash.

This kind of seller has many names, but I call him a flexible seller, or a motivated seller. By "motivated" I mean that his motive for selling is something other than to get his hands on a lot of cash.

We tend to assume that all sellers of property need cash. But it isn't true. Some sellers need cash, but not all do.

Sellers who urgently need money aren't very flexible about it; they can't afford to be. Your first job is to separate the flexible sellers from the inflexible, and avoid wasting your time with the latter.

Seven Kinds of Flexible Seller

Almost all flexible sellers have one thing in common. They are people in transition. A change is occurring in their lives. The change has made them want to get rid of their property soon.

Whenever you find one of the following situations, you may find a property owner from whom you can buy without putting up much cash:

    A. Divorce
    B. Job transfer
    C. Loss of job
    D. Retirement
    E. Smaller family
        (children grown up and moved out)
    F. Death in family
    G. Absentee ownership

The above list contains people who have trauma in their lives. Don't create more. You needn't take advantage of people to make money. You can make plenty of money in real estate by treating people fairly.

Your attitude should be that you'll find a way to meet the needs of other people as well as yourself—a win/win solution, as it's called. Both parties get what they need —nobody loses. The seller names the price, you name the terms. Each wins. Then forever afterward you can go out to lunch with people from whom you've bought, and enjoy yourself, because you haven't taken advantage of them. Nor have they skinned you. If you get rid of a winner/loser attitude, you can enjoy life at the same time that you're making money.

Later in the book I'll give you all the mechanics of working out transactions with these people—but let's take a moment now to consider each type briefly.

A. Divorce. After a break-up, whoever gets the house may not want to stay there and may not have any pressing need for extra cash. How do you find such a person?

By looking at divorce notices, which are filed at the county courthouse. A brief letter expressing interest in purchasing the home might turn up a win/win solution.

B. Job transfer. Many of these are sudden. If a family must move to another city, they probably need to sell their property quickly. (Of course, if they need a hefty sum for a down payment on a home in the new location, they're not for you. But some families don't, because they plan to rent.) Maybe the husband has already left for the new job, and the wife must stay behind until she sells. She wants the family reunited as soon as possible. Your offer of a quick closing may be the key to transaction.

C. Loss of job. An unemployed breadwinner may need to get out from under the house payments quickly. Offer to close before the next payment is due.

D. Retirement. Many retirees decide to move. They want a better climate, or they want to be nearer their children, or maybe they just feel restless for other reasons. Most retired couples want a steady income to live on, not a big lump of cash. A "No Down Payment" sale may give them everything they want.

E. The "empty nest" syndrome is a good reason to sell a big house and move to a smaller one, or to an apartment. Again, the owners very likely don't need cash.

F. Death. Dad was a whiz at real estate. Mom isn't— or vice versa. The survivor wants to get rid of property worries, and in many cases will carry a mortgage. Notices of estate sales are good leads to prospective flexible sellers.

G. Any of the above kinds of change may create a situation where a property is owned by someone living hundreds of miles away, or farther. Absentee owners are much more likely to want to sell than local owners. The addresses of out-of-state owners are on the property tax rolls at the courthouse. Write to as many as you can. If their property doesn't look good (overgrown lawn, peel-

ing paint) all the more reason they'll want to unload it—
so take a snapshot and send it along. Minor cosmetics
are easily corrected.

Clues in the Classified Ads

When you write to individuals like those I've just
listed, you may find motivated sellers who haven't been
approached by anyone else. But you need time to write
letters, and more time while you wait for answers. Meanwhile there's a fast way to spot other prospects who've
already put their property on the market and can be in-
duced to sell for little or no cash.

Just pick up whatever major newspaper is published
closest to where you live. Turn to the real-estate section.
There you'll find hundreds of homes and buildings advertised for sale.

Some of these properties can be bought with a minimum down payment or nothing down. How can you spot
them? Mainly by skimming the words in big type at the
beginning of the ads.

For example, you really will find occasional ads
headed NOTHING DOWN. There's a clue! There are
others with variations, like LOW DOWN PAYMENT
. . . LOW–LOW DOWN . . . $1,000 . . . $2,000 DOWN.

Jump on these the minute you see them. If the owner
is serious, they won't last long—and you know they're
being offered by the kind of owner you can negotiate
with. You and this owner have already reached agreement on the most important factor: Little or no down
payment. All that's left is to agree on the terms. (Price?
You're willing to give him his price, *if* you can get your
terms.)

Watch for Hints from Owners

As I've already implied, an important part of your
buying strategy is to persuade a seller to lend you most

or all of the purchase price, at below-market interest. In other words, he must "carry back the paper," as real-estate people say.

If an owner isn't willing to carry back financing he isn't a motivated seller—so what are you doing there?

Also, his equity in the property should be high. I like it to be 25 percent or more.

A motivated seller may not openly proclaim that he'll listen to no-cash buyers, because he's heard that it's always best to get a hefty down payment; and besides it would be a nice feeling to have that crisp check in his hand, even if he doesn't need it. But if he's really motivated, he may drop hints, even in the headline of his ad —like OWNER FINANCING . . . FLEXIBLE FINANCING . . . OWC (owner will carry) . . . OWNER WILL PARTICIPATE IN FINANCING, or other words to that effect.

If an owner will take your note for the purchase price, and also has an existing FHA or VA loan, this combination can easily lead to a low down and low payment transaction—which of course would be an especially attractive investment. (You can easily assume FHA government-backed loans, at the original low interest rate, without any credit check.) So watch for ads that mention "existing government loan" or some other reference to FHA or VA.

FOR SALE BY OWNER is another headliner hint, although it isn't surefire. The Fizbo (FSBO) as it's known in the real-estate trade, may or may not be for sale on flexible terms. But I think it's always worth a call. Use the telephone-approach techniques in Chapter 6 to find out whether or not the owner is the type you're looking for.

Also worth a call are many other ads with headlines that tell you the seller has a strong urge to sell quickly. These include OWNER MUST SELL . . . BRING ANY OFFER . . . PRICED BELOW MARKET VALUE . . .

DISTRESS SALE BY OWNER . . . REDUCED FOR
QUICK SALE . . . FAST SALE WANTED . . . EASY
TO BUY . . . and so on.

All the preceding, by the way, are actual headlines I
found in a local newspaper. So don't let anyone tell you
that flexible sellers are scarcer than strawberries in Si-
beria. They do turn up every few days. Look at the
weekend papers and you'll see.

One ad I didn't see, but just heard about, was a clas-
sic: I'M DOWN, KICK ME. I believe it only ran once.
There was enough to bring more would-be buyers than
the advertiser needed.

My point is simply this. Golden opportunities are
yours for the seeking. It's worth investing a few hours a
week to find them.

But here's a further point. Narrow down the area in
which you follow up leads.

Take a map of the area in which you live, stick a pin
in your house and draw a circle around it representing a
fifty-mile area. I'd like to see you build your financial
independence inside that circle. Your progress will be
faster. Within fifty miles of your home you can probably
find any kind of property you might want to invest in.
Big, small, expensive, cheap—anything you want.

By limiting your search area you won't spend so
much time driving back and forth to see owners. Also,
after you take title to a property, you should be able to
visit it and return home in a few hours. This almost guarantees that you *will* visit the property often, thereby
keeping in touch with neighborhood changes and local
business conditions.

A third reason for the fifty-mile limit is that lenders
get nervous about dealing with a borrower who lives outside their own area, especially if he has very little net
worth. Later on, when you have a net worth of $200,000
or so, you can buy property in Phoenix, Denver, Florida
or wherever. Even if you live in Chicago or Keokuk, if

you are in Phoenix trying to get a loan from a lender, he'll be all smiles if you put a half-million-dollar financial statement in front of him. Likewise, you'll be able to afford property managers to look after distant investments.

Car Cruising Can Pay Off

Why not get in your car next Saturday or Sunday and drive slowly around the most promising neighborhoods within easy distance of your home? (Remember, in the previous chapter I advised buying in middle-class or upper-middle neighborhoods if you invest in one-family homes.) Watch for signs saying FOR SALE BY OWNER. Many of these aren't advertised in the newspaper.

A variation of this (and it's tougher) is to stop whenever you see people outside working on their lawn. Saunter up and say something like "I'm looking to buy a home. Do you know anyone who's thinking of selling?" If they mention someone, thank them, get their name to mention, then look up the prospect in the phone book and call. Your basic approach can be the standard one I'll explain in Chapter 7. It shouldn't take you long to determine whether the owner does or doesn't have a need for cash.

Come-Hither in Cards

There are many other ways to find sellers. In fact, sellers will come looking for you if you invest a little money in business cards—and if you get the cards into circulation.

How many times have you been at a party or some other get-together and been asked, "What do you do?" Stop answering "I make therapeutic shoelaces," or whatever your occupation is. If you're going to be a real-estate investor, get yourself known as a real-estate investor. Order some business cards you can hand out.

HOLLIS NORTON
REAL ESTATE INVESTOR

I buy homes, apartments, commercial properties

444-2222
P. O. Box 7777
Any City, Any State

Don't order cheap cards. Get the best—stiff cardboard, engraved and all that, with a type style that implies solid business. (Ask the printer to show you typography used by executives of well-known corporations.)

A good-looking business card impresses people. Make yours memorable but not flashy. Pass them out whenever you're asked the "What do you do" question —or when you're not.

Keep circulating. Spread the word about your new business throughout your network of relatives, friends and acquaintances. Wherever you go, stay alert. Listen to the conversation, and occasionally you'll pick up on a mention of someone's upcoming need to sell. There's nothing wrong with building future wealth for yourself at the same time you're being social.

Make sure all your cousins, nephews, in-laws and old school chums know that you buy real estate. The larger your family, and the wider your circle of acquaintances, the more contacts. People would normally rather sell for no down payment to a friend or relative than to a stranger.

Ladies, a word of caution. Don't put your home address on your business cards you pass out en masse, for obvious reasons. Use your business address. If you don't have one yet, get a post office box (easy to rent) for an address.

Better yet for either sex, turn yourself into a conglomerate for only a few dollars' application fee. That is, acquire a DBA (Doing Business As—) name. It's easy. Just go down to the courthouse and register the business name you select.

Your DBA is only a fictitious name, but it's legal and it sure can sound impressive. For example, if you live in California or Arizona or Texas or thereabouts, your DBA might be "Great Southwestern Properties." Sounds like you're in business in several states, doesn't it?

Use expensive stationery with your DBA on the letterhead, and with envelopes to match. This gives you an air of wealth and success without actually having attained it yet. Your business card might read:

GREAT SOUTHWESTERN PROPERTIES

Address

Your Own Name

Property Acquisition   Phone Number(s)

Your Ad Can Attract Sellers

Do you want ten or twelve sellers calling you every week? Just invest a few dollars in a classified ad, to run regularly in the real estate wanted column. You might head it NOTHING DOWN, with some brief descriptive copy underneath and your phone number. Then your phone will start ringing.

The ad I got the most response from was this:

WILL PAY FULL PRICE FOR YOUR

PROPERTY IF YOU WILL SELL ON

FLEXIBLE TERMS

(little or nothing down)

CALL HOLLIS AT

888-9999

When someone calls on that ad, you already *know* they are willing to sell without a cash down payment. So you're off to a beautiful start. The sale is half made already.

Join Your Way to Wealth

Join the local Apartment Owners Association and form friendships. Friends like to sell to friends.

Pay attention to the more neglected members—the *older* ones. After all, who is likely to sell his or her property soonest? Someone getting ready to retire, that's who.

And who is more inclined to think in terms of steady income rather than cash, than someone ready to retire? Ask such people for fatherly advice. Invite them to dinner.

Okay, I've given you a flock of ideas to start with. But don't limit yourself to what you've just read. Put your own mind to work inventing ways to locate motivated sellers. Just as you build muscles by working out in a gym, you build brainpower by exercising your mind. The more you stimulate the creative areas in your cranium, the more ideas you'll think of.

Remember: The greatest money-making machine is between your ears. Use it and build wealth!

6

HOW TO TALK WITH SELLERS

LET'S SUPPOSE YOU'VE BEEN SYSTEMATICALLY CAN-
vassing newspapers, public records and other sources for
sellers who might be flexible about down payment and
terms. Every day you've written a few letters. Maybe
you've advertised.

As it always will, this methodical searching has
brought results. You've begun to find people who may
be willing to sell on your terms.

So now it's time to get ready for the next steps: first,
approaching those people by phone; second, talking further with whichever ones indicate that they really are
flexible.

What should you say during these steps? How should
you handle yourself? That's what this chapter is about.

You're a Salesman

I'll begin by laying some groundwork. The first thing
to realize is that the job ahead of you is a *selling* job. Not
a high-pressure sales job, but a job of selling yourself.

Oh, sure, you want to *buy* property. But you've got
to convince the other person that he or she will benefit
by helping you buy on your terms. In that sense, you're
a salesman—as we all are (or should be) in every spot
where we need to win someone's cooperation. So the
time-tested principles of good selling apply here.

The first principle: a good salesperson needs *confidence*. You probably won't have it at first. But it gets easier with every approach you make. The hardest approach is the first. Before you phone that first owner, your throat may go dry, your hands perspire, your knees wobble. The second one, you're not quite so nervous. The tenth one is a lay-down.

You have to realize that you won't be me when you start—you'll be me minus practice. I didn't transform into me, I grew into me, owner by owner by owner. Owners don't get any stronger—you do.

I've known people who made it in a tougher kind of selling than you're about to try: door-to-door selling. They all went through terror. At their first calls they could hardly pump up enough courage to push the doorbell. As one of them said, "I knew that when the ring was answered, I'd face a stranger whom I would have to ask to buy something. My fear sent a message to the potential customer. She found it easy to say, 'Not today, thanks.'"

After a few weeks of getting no after no, these salesmen had another experience in common: "The idea hit me like a landslide," one said. "I wasn't out asking for favors. I was trying to sell people something it was clearly in their interest to buy. Once I was sold on this, prospects weren't fearsome."

So the first person you have to convince is yourself. A convert is always the strongest salesman for his cause. Why? Because he is so sold on it that he wants everybody else to benefit, too. He's a man with a mission. His enthusiasm comes across.

How can you get steamed up like this? By realizing what you can do for the people you approach. The drive that puts steam into selling anything (a product, a proposition, an idea) is the knowledge that we're honestly doing the other guy a service. We're offering something he can't afford to turn down. Stop feeling like he's doing you a favor.

To get yourself into this enthusiastic frame of mind, you need to understand fully how your way of buying can help the people who sell to you. Maybe you need to read this whole book before you're completely convinced. If so, okay. For now, let's assume that you fully understand your proposition. You're ready to explain all its ramifications to anyone who can benefit from it.

Now for the approach. After any salesman is convinced that his proposition is good to start with, he must make sure he aims it at the right person. Salespeople call this step "qualifying the prospect," or "screening." Promotion people call it "finding selling opportunities." Whatever it's called, it's essential.

Who is a prospect? A prospect is someone in a situation that makes him likely to buy what the salesman is selling. Someone with a need which the salesman can satisfy. In your case, a person whose need to sell exceeds his need for cash.

Be Sure You're Talking to the Right Person

You wouldn't try to sell dog food to someone who has no dog. You wouldn't try to borrow money from someone who's broke. So you won't try to buy property from people who really need a hefty down payment. They aren't "qualified." Your proposition wouldn't help them.

The purpose of your approach by phone is to confirm that Mr. Seller is qualified—that he's motivated, flexible —as I explained in the last chapter. Don't assume he is. Find out. That way, when you actually ask for an appointment, you'll know you won't be wasting his time or yours. You'll be stepping into a "buying opportunity."

Even when a seller is qualified, don't start negotiating during your first phone conversation. Why? Because half of all communication is personal appearance and facial expressions and body language. Nothing beats sitting down with the seller face to face (regardless of what the real-estate brokers may tell you).

For emphasis, I repeat: the purpose of the phone call is not to agree on a purchase. It is only to qualify the seller as someone willing to sell for very little cash down. Okay—so what should you say on the phone?

You start by identifying yourself. People hesitate to answer questions from just a strange voice on the phone. So you say, "Hi, this is (your name). I understand you are selling your property."

Make your voice warm and friendly. But not too loud or fast, because that sounds like high pressure. Try to smile while you're speaking, even though the other person can't see you. It affects your own mood, and it makes your voice more friendly.

If the person doesn't volunteer his name, ask for it. Then use it in every sentence or two. People like to hear their names. Unless this particular Mr. or Mrs. Seller sounds especially formal, you can say something like, "Just call me Joe. May I call you Tom?" Shifting to a first-name basis helps establish rapport.

Get Them Talking Freely

If the seller doesn't offer information about the house right away, ask him, "Can you tell me a little about the house?"

Listen to everything the seller says. Good salespeople sell by listening as well as talking. There may be information that you can use later when you're face to face. Even if not, even if this seller just rambles, pay close attention. People like to have attention paid. They prefer to deal with someone who is interested in them. The better *listener* you become, the more real estate you'll buy.

Pleasantly and patiently, you can steer a rambler back on course. Just say, when he slows down, "Can you tell me more about . . . ?" or "Would you go into more detail on . . . ?"

Take notes. If you get behind on your note-taking, catch up by injecting a question such as "You said three bedrooms, right?"

Now for the Key Questions

When the above phase is over, it's time for an important question: "Why are you selling the property?"

Really listen to the answer. Sometimes sellers will hint or admit that they don't need cash. Example: "We've bought another home. We're going to move and we don't need this one." Conclusion: They don't need cash for a down payment, because they have *already* purchased their next home.

Or maybe their answer reveals that they're hard-pressed for cash. If they *haven't* bought their next house yet, they probably want enough for the usual 25 percent down. But don't jump to conclusions. Verify your guess by saying something like "Sounds like you may need a substantial down payment. How much were you figuring on?"

If you see that someone is definitely not a low-cash-down seller, explain politely that his terms are out of your reach, thank him and hang up. Dial the next number. You're entering a very profitable business. But it isn't a business where every call you make gets the kind of answer you want. Think of it as a new version of "Dialing For Dollars."

Sometimes the answer to "Why are you selling?" doesn't tell you whether or not the seller needs cash. Okay. You've now been on the phone for a few minutes, the seller has warmed up, and you can ask an even more important question. Ask it casually: "If you can get your price, do you have any need for a lot of cash?"

If the answer is no, you need to make an appointment. "Great, why don't I stop by this evening and see if we can't put this together?" (If it's already evening, make the appointment for the next evening—or during the day if this would be convenient for both of you.)

Sometimes you're phoning someone whose ad says "Low Down." Then you don't ask the question about needing a lot of cash. Instead, just verify that the seller means what the ad said. Then go on and make the appointment.

Then add a little bonus: "If we can agree on terms, would a ten-day closing be too soon for you?"

Let the seller start to think of the property as sold. That will sink in between the time you talk on the telephone and the time you arrive at the house.

Before you hang up, ask about the existing mortgage on the property. You'll need this information to structure an offer (see section "Writing the Offer" in Chapter 11). Arrive at the seller's home with a written offer for, say, a thousand dollars down (less if you don't have that much).

When You Visit a Seller

Right or wrong, people judge you visually: by the clothes on your back, the car you drive, your grooming and manners and all that. "What you are speaks so loudly, I cannot hear what you say," somebody famous (I don't remember who) remarked long ago.

So it's up to you to look your best. All good salespeople do.

Buy yourself one good suit (male) or business suit or dress (female). Nothing extreme. Black pinstripe or dark blue is best. That one good suit or dress will more than earn its keep.

What about your car? In most major cities there are agencies that rent Cadillacs. For just a few hours, it's not that expensive. Think about it. When was the last time you asked a guy in an expensive suit driving a Cadillac if he had money or not? (Remember, you'll be asking for a loan—that is, you'll ask the seller to lend his equity in the property.)

If this isn't feasible and you have an older car (especially one with dents), set your appointments for after dark and park down the street. You still want to wear your best clothes. Needless to say, your grooming will be impeccable.

Whatever you do, make sure to be on time. Promptness is part of good salesmanship. So is courtesy.

You're There to Help

So is helpfulness. In fact, helpfulness is the most important part of salesmanship. Soon after you arrive, it's a good idea to say something like "Mr. Seller, I don't really buy property anymore, I solve problems for sellers. If I can help you, I'll buy your property. If not, I won't."

And then sit there and help that human being to the best of your ability, with all your heart, mind and soul.

Do this every time you call on a seller and you'll find yourself getting wealthy (funny about that). Win/win works. Another benefit is, you will start to feel very good about yourself. (It's hard to enjoy money, or life, if you don't.)

Sometimes you'll arrive to find that a prospect isn't ready to talk because something unexpected has come up. This may be your chance to forget business and be helpful in other ways. Fine.

Betty Barner, a highly successful canvasser for cemetery lots, once told of some of her experiences in *The American Salesman* magazine:

> I arrived at one home to find a mother
> frantic because she had no one to sit with

her three children while she went on an
important errand. I became baby-sitter
for an hour.

I have pitched in to help a harassed
housewife clean up and wash the dishes.
I have done marketing for the sick. Once
I prepared a baby's formula.

Out of all this, I have become known
as "Friend Betty" in many a home, and
when these people are ready to talk business, they naturally turn to their
"Friend."

Sitting Down with the Seller

Anyhow, let's say the time has come to talk business.
Still nervous? No reason to be. You can expect a friendly
listener. As you made clear over the phone, you're there
to give him his price. You're probably going to show him
a better way to sell. Unlike others who may talk to him,
you don't have to crank his price down, which in many
cases, makes a seller hostile.

"You name the price, I'll name the terms," you can
say. "This property is worth $150,000 and you're going
to get it. Let me show you how I can give it to you."

What's he going to say? Don't show me? I never
heard anybody say that. They may not like what you
show them, but everybody sits there and listens. And
don't take the no's personally. There are too many good
prospects for you to be bothered when one turns out not
to be good.

Always try to put yourself in the seller's place. Ask
yourself, "How would I feel if I were in his shoes? What
would I be thinking?"

Don't be a blabbermouth. Many people kill a purchase by talking too much. Stick to the point. Make it
simple and short.

And watch for feedback. Are you getting your points across? Few people are good listeners. Often they hear, but they forget. Or they don't believe you because they don't understand.

Does Everybody Understand?

This is a problem when you explain a real-estate proposition to owners who maybe haven't ever talked real estate in their lives. Jargon scares them. If you say "equity" or "financing" or "carry-back paper," they may not know what you mean, and be too embarrassed to say so.

Even a simple phrase can have different meanings to different people, including you. Think about "pretty little girl's bedroom." Is the room pretty? Or is the girl pretty? Is the room little, or is it a little girl? Is there one girl, or are there more than one?

Count von Moltke, a great military organizer, told his generals (all very smart men), "Remember, gentlemen, anything which can be misunderstood *will* be misunderstood." It's still true. Make sure you and the seller understand each other.

Good negotiators keep asking questions to see if there's any misunderstanding. One good question is, "Did I make that clear, or does it sound confusing?" Another is, "Let's see if I understand. In other words . . ."

How's your tact? *Never* say, "You misunderstood," or "I guess you don't get what I'm saying" or even "My advice to you is . . ." And never seem to be arguing. An argument is a clash of egos. If you show up the other guy and shoot his argument full of holes, you'll feel big. But he'll feel inferior. And he'll probably never sell to you. Remember: "A man convinced against his will is of the same opinion still."

Dale Carnegie, who ran famous training programs for

salesmen, put the same point another way: "No one likes
to feel he is being sold something. We much prefer to
feel that we are buying of our own accord and not being
'sold.' We like to be consulted about our wishes, our
wants, our thoughts."

You may be very close to buying an investment with
no cash—and lose it because you jump to conclusions
instead of asking questions.

Example: You walk into a seller's house. You have
no cash. You say to him, "What do you want for a down
payment?" He tells you, "I don't need much. All I need
is one thousand down and I will carry back the balance."
You think you almost found him, but you don't have the
thousand, so you walk out. Or, if you're smarter, you sit
there and ask, "What do you plan to do with the down
payment?"

He may say he's going to buy some furniture for his
new house, that's all. Take him down to your Sears
store, where you have a charge account. Let him charge
a thousand dollars' worth of furniture on your account.
You make easy monthly payments on your account, and
you've bought the house for nothing down. You bought
because you *didn't* reach a conclusion—you asked another question.

Learn to Close

No one has to be a supersalesman to buy a lot of real
estate. But it helps to learn one more basic principle: how
to "close"—how to pop the big question and get the
seller's signature.

People don't like to decide. So they put it off. Why
hurry? Maybe a better offer will come along. They'll
think about it. They'll talk it over with So-and-so. They
won't act unless they're nudged.

There's a fable about a mule that starved to death
because he couldn't decide which stack of straw to eat

first. The fable means that some people lose out because
they can't make up their minds. This is an old story to
salesmen, so they watch for chances to get a yes. When
the time seems ripe, they push for a decision—in a low-
pressure way.

Maybe they say, "Shall I send this to your house or
your office? . . . Will you charge this, or would you
rather pay cash? . . . Shall I put *Rush* on this order?"
They act *as if* the prospect has made up his mind.

You don't want to sit there all night and play objection–answer, objection–answer. Sometimes it is simply
a matter of overcoming a final objection in order to buy
a lot of real estate.

The simplest way to close, when you're asked a question for which you have a good answer (I'll give you
some in a moment), is to try to make that question the
final objection. Say: "If I can satisfy you on this, do we
have a deal?"

Wait for a nod. When you get it, give the answer and
shake hands. But don't leave anything dangling. To some
people, a nod and handshake may be just stalling. The
next morning they may call up, and say they have
thought it over, and are sorry, but they've decided to
wait awhile.

The only yes that finally counts is the one followed
by a signature. Early in the negotiations you should un-
obtrusively pull out the papers and put them in plain
sight. Then there won't be the awkward pause that might
come when you stopped and fumbled for the papers after
the handshake. And the seller gets used to looking at
them. He won't be frightened by them when the time
comes to sign.

Have the pen ready, and the dotted line marked with
a red X. But don't say "Sign here." That's scary. Instead say something like "Be sure to write your name
just as it's typed below," or "While you're filling this in,
I can make out my check."

Objections and Possible Answers

Sellers often have fears about selling their property with little or no cash down. The following are some of the fears, expressed as questions. I've included answers after the questions.

Remember, you *are* going to pay your debt. Let your sincerity show through in your answers. I'm not talking about taking advantage of people. This is a win/win concept of real-estate investing. You win and the seller wins. He gets his price. You get your terms.

The answers below are not engraved on tablets. They are not necessarily the final word. They are meant as guidelines for you. You are also allowed to use the common sense the good Lord gave you.

Question: "How do I know you'll pay me?"

(Note: For answer number 1 to work, you must have bought at least one other property and your payments must have been prompt.)

Answer number 1: "I've had many people ask me that question and you have a right to be concerned. That's why I carry this list with me. Here are the people I've bought property from. Their phone numbers are there. Why don't you call one or two and ask them how I pay?"

Answer number 2 (if you own another property): "I'll tell you what. I own a lot in Death Valley. It has _____ thousand dollars in equity. I'll give you a mortgage on the land (a blanket mortgage—one that covers a group of properties), and after I've proved myself by making, say, twelve payments, you release my lot."

Answer number 3 (if you have never bought, or don't now own property): "Here is a copy of my credit report. As you can see, I have paid my bills promptly for many years. You can also see there are no foreclosures." (TRW—see page 95—will sell you a copy of your credit report for a few dollars.)

Answer number 4 (if you have no property, bad credit, and want to own your first home): "There is one thing my wife wants and that's her own home. If I have to get an extra job and eat bread and water, that payment is going to be made. Nobody is going to take away her home!" Again, let your sincerity show through.

Question: "Why should I sell this way?" (Low or no down payment.)

Answer: "The problem you have, Mr. Seller, is you want to sell this property fairly quickly, right? Real estate takes time to sell. If you're going to sell quickly and get a lot of cash, you have to discount your property. You pay a terrible price to get cash. The beautiful part of my proposal is that you get your price and still sell quickly."

Question: "Why should I accept the low interest rate you offer when I can get more in a bank certificate or a money-market fund?"

Answer: "I think this is a general area of confusion, Mr. Seller. Many people don't realize that there's a difference between the hard-money market (where you borrow against your home and get cash), and seller financing. A hard-money loan is a businessman renting cash for a rate that's set in the marketplace. A seller carry-back loan is an inducement by the seller to get the buyer to purchase. Seller financing is always at a much lower rate than conventional financing."

Spend some time practicing the answers in this chapter with your wife, husband or a friend until you become comfortable with them. This will really help when you're sitting down with sellers.

Sometimes a seller just won't sign until he's consulted his attorney. In that case I would try to arrange a meeting with him and the attorney together, so I can feed some positive inputs to offset the attorney's negative inputs. Many lawyers take the view that the world doesn't work —everything is negative. They'd rather make a living stirring things up than quieting them down. They tend to get more fees that way.

Work to get the attorney on your side at the same time you give the appearance he is earning his fee. If you antagonize him, he will talk the seller out of the deal after you've gone.

7

HOW MUCH
IS THIS PROPERTY
WORTH?

I KNOW MANY OF YOU ARE HOPING TO FIND A NICE magic formula to tell what your property is worth. Sorree–e–e. It's just not that simple. There are more variables in pricing real estate than you can count—everything from the better-known rules of thumb (generally unreliable) to the most famous of all valuation systems, PFA. What is PFA? Why, Picked From Air, of course.

I'm going to give you some ideas in this chapter. The first thing I want you to do is not to give yourself an impossible task. Don't say, "I'm going to become an expert on the value of real estate in the city of Chicago" (or wherever you live). The bigger the city, the more impossible the task. You would find yourself spending all your time keeping up with prices, and no time writing offers. Let's break it down a little. I want you to buy property in middle- to upper-middle-class neighborhoods. We don't want the extremes. We don't want Beverly Hills and we don't want the ghetto. It's very difficult to rent properties in Beverly Hills for enough money for you to make the payments. At the other end, if I need a guard dog and a gorilla to collect my rents, I'm not interested. A good evaluator for a neighborhood is, Would I be comfortable in the area after dark? If the answer is yes, that's probably a good place to invest.

Let's pick a quadrant of your city that has such neighborhoods. Southeast, Northwest, it doesn't matter. I would like you to narrow even further to one or two neighborhoods. If you live in that kind of neighborhood, yours and one other is a good place to start. If you live in a poorer or richer area, you won't be buying where you live. That's not a major inconvenience.

Now, let's look at how to tell what a property is worth. The easiest properties to work with are single-family homes and small apartment buildings. Let me give you a simple way to get a good feel for prices. Any local realtor or broker who is a member of the multiple listing service (MLS) has a SOLD book. This is the one you never hear about. It's not the normal MLS book; that's the listing book. We don't want to know what they list for. We want to know what they sell for. Go in a local office and say, "I want to buy some properties in this area. I'd like to look at your SOLD book to get an idea what prices homes are selling for." Sit down at a desk and look at three-bedroom two-bath homes (nice rentals) to your heart's content. If you get resistance about using the book, don't fight—walk down the street to the next broker. However, not too many brokers are going to throw a potential buyer out of their offices.

Note that the MLS book and the SOLD book also contain apartment buildings (mostly smaller ones). This will give you an idea of what these buildings sell for also.

Let's take a look at income property. You're going to find a large number of rules of thumb in the marketplace. They are useful in determining an approximate value of property. You can be badly burned if you take one of these rules of thumb and use it to buy buildings. Let's look at just a few of them and what some of the problems are.

1. X times the gross income. You will hear that in the marketplace buildings sell for 8 X, 10 X, 12 X the gross income, or whatever the multiple is in the particular area of your city. The main problem in buying times gross is that the expenses of buildings can vary greatly. Let's

take one example: utilities on the buildings. Who pays for them, the tenant or the landlord? Is the building individually metered so that the tenant pays, or on a central system so that the landlord pays? Also, when the landlord pays, tenants tend not to conserve and bills can be very high. You might end up paying 10 to 15 percent of the gross for utilities. This reduces the value of the building even though times gross doesn't take this into account.

2. X times the net income. This is supposed to solve the problem of times gross. The net income is the gross income of the building minus the expenses (not debt service). You then pay 8, 10, 12 times the net, or whatever is fair where you live. The main objection to this is, if you use the income-expense sheet the real-estate broker gives you to estimate expenses, you could have serious problems. The broker prepares the form based on expenses supplied by the seller. Sellers do not overestimate expenses; they are noted for sins of omission. You can, for one thing, have the seller guarantee in writing that the expenses are accurately stated. Let me give you a better way. Ask to see the page of his last year's tax return that relates to the building (the K-1 form—the form that lists all the expenses). He may lie to you, but it's unlikely, since all expenses are tax-deductible, that he's going to omit anything on that income-tax return. I will also show you later in the book a fairly accurate way to determine the expenses of a building.

3. Appraised value. Many investors look to pay at or below the appraised value of a property. Some say, "I never pay over X percent of the appraised value." There are problems with using only appraisals. One, appraisals vary greatly. Two, you don't take into account terms. Let's say a building is appraised for $100,000. I may pay anywhere from $80,000 (all cash) to $110,000 (very, very soft terms). Appraisals, however, can prevent you from grossly overpaying for a property.

What does all this mean? Well, here's what I do. I
look at a property from a standpoint of: Will it carry
itself? Is the owner flexible about terms? If he will let me
use some of the "eliminate negative cash flow" methods
described later in this book, I am not too picky about
price. I don't sell real estate—I just buy it. I know that
many years down the road, when that property has doubled, even tripled, in value, I won't care that I supposedly paid a few thousand too much for it. At the same
time I want you to use the multipliers, appraisals, etc.,
to verify that you're "in the ballpark" pricewise. Listen
carefully. Even if you make an occasional mistake and
overpay, time is a great healer. Remember the general
rule that prices over the long term keep going up.

8

TWENTY-TWO WAYS TO BUY IF YOU'RE CASH POOR

MOST OWNERS HOPE TO GET A BIG DOWN PAYMENT when they sell their property. Since you don't have it, you must be able to suggest alternatives. Carry around a mental tool kit of solutions to financing problems.

I hope you'll study this chapter closely. Read and reread it until all twenty-two of its techniques are permanently in your mind, so that you can run through them mentally as if scanning a checklist whenever you're talking with someone who may be a flexible seller. Be ready to suggest various ideas that might fit his needs as well as your own.

Don't forget to "qualify" a seller before you start making offers. (Review Chapter 6 for the key questions to ask at the beginning of a conversation.) When someone really is in urgent need of a big hunk of cash, you'd be wasting his time and yours by suggesting the buying methods described below (with an occasional exception for numbers 3, 5, 12, 13, 14, 15 or 19). Most of these twenty-two methods are designed to give you 95 percent leverage or more. They'll also give the seller the full price he wants, if he can afford to let you pay slowly.

Keep in mind what I've mentioned often in previous chapters: We're talking about *income* property that you'll plan to hold a long time. If you want to buy property on speculation and let it sit vacant while you maneuver for profitable resale, you're reading the wrong book.

My philosophy of investing is to control property *and the income from it* without using much cash, so that its monthly revenues will more than cover your monthly debt payments as well as any up-front costs such as fees to a lawyer, appraiser, broker or others.

With that understood, let's run through the list. Then you can get ready to keep making purchase offers until a flexible seller accepts one.

1. The Lease-Option¨

I'll go into this in greater detail in Chapter 14, but you should be aware of it now, because it's a beautiful way to buy a home with no cash and no credit.

Lease a house under an agreement that a part of the monthly lease payment (try for half or more) will apply toward the down payment on the house if you exercise your option to buy it.

A three-year lease (or longer) is best. When the lease period expires, you buy your house, as permitted by the option you took in the beginning.

Down payment? Already taken care of. It comes from your monthly payment (about as much as you might have been paying in apartment rent elsewhere).

The owner's mortgage? You assume it at the end of the lease. The difference between what's due on this mortgage and what you're paying for the house will be borrowed from the seller in the form of a second mortgage.

Since the house will almost certainly go up in value during the lease period, there's a built-in profit that you can take later by refinancing or selling the property. Always put in a right to sublet. If it's not your home, you want a tenant to make the payments for you.

2. Installment Down Payment

Say you wanted a house, but you didn't have the $3,000 the owner was asking for a down payment. You offer to make the down payment in installments, in addition to the monthly payments.

Example: A $65,000 house for sale. Payment on house you are buying is $650. You pay $750 for 30 months. The extra $100 per month for the 30 months would make up the $3,000 down payment. You pay for the down payment in installments much the way you buy your car.

3. Family and Friend Loans

Sit down and make a list of people who know and like you—relatives, neighbors, friends, customers and so on. They are all potential sources of loans.

Ask them what rate of interest they are currently receiving on their savings. Offer them 1 or 2 percent more. Remember, a great source of collateral to them would be a second or third mortgage on the property you are buying.

If these interest payments to your family or friends, plus the current mortgage payments on the property, add up to a net overflow of cash each month, review Chapter 11 for ways of avoiding negative cash flow.

4. 100 Percent Financing

This is what I call the mortgage-out technique. It's another beautiful way to buy a property. Take over the existing financing on a property and get the seller to carry back an additional mortgage for all of his equity. Obviously, he'll have to be much more concerned about unloading the property quickly than about the cash he'll be receiving. Negotiate as small payments on his equity as he is willing to accept.

5. Private Loan

When you need extra cash for a down payment, advertise for it!

Believe it or not, your local newspaper is one of the best sources of money. Run an ad and ask for it.

Almost every major paper has a classified section headed "Money Wanted." In order to get a lot of calls, avoid being too specific. Your ad might read:

NEED $10,000 SECURED BY

QUALITY REAL ESTATE

BILL, 849-6271

When someone calls, explain what you are looking for. If the caller says no, ask him what kind of real estate he does lend on. Get his phone number and start a card file. You may run across something later that would make money for both of you.

To induce a private lender to make the loan, you can offer a sweetener—a percentage of the profits down the road (no more than 10 percent) when you sell the property or refinance it. This doesn't cost you anything. There *are* no profits if you can't put a transaction together.

Warning: Since not everyone is completely honest, be sure you have the property tied up on a contract before you tell the lender its address or other details that would enable him to find it and buy it himself.

6. Anything for a Down Payment

A down payment doesn't always have to be in cash. To certain sellers, a second-hand car or boat or some other possession of yours may be just as acceptable as money. Think over the things you own (including those that aren't totally paid off) and see what you can offer in lieu of cash. (I'll discuss this in more detail in the next chapter.)

Sometimes a combination offer of cash-plus-property will make it more attractive. Example:

$6,000 down payment
$5,000 equity in a boat (describe fully)
$1,000 cash

7. Blanket Mortgage

A blanket mortgage is a mortgage on more than one property (not the same as a wraparound mortgage, which is a mortgage on a property subordinate to, yet including, all the encumbrances to which it is subordinated). Its purpose is to increase the collateral (security) behind the loan. This is a good way of inducing the seller to take your offer.

One use of the blanket mortgage would be to combine it with number 4, the mortgage-out technique. Suppose the seller shows concern about whether you'll make the monthly payments. To quiet his fears, you offer to let the second mortgage he'll carry back cover both the house he's selling you and something else you own (a lot you bought and can't sell is a good candidate). This shows him that he'll definitely come out ahead if he has to foreclose.

Be sure and put a clause into the agreement releasing the other property after twelve to twenty-four payments have been made—the exact number of payments to be made before release is negotiable.

8. Raise the Price, Better the Terms

Appeal to one of the seller's finer points—his human greed. Along with your very low down payment, offer him a little more for his property than he's asking. It's a very effective way to cushion the shock of your proposal to lower the down payment. It works very well in negotiations with sellers who've been advertising one of these two offers:

A. "Reduced for quick sale" ads

Tell the seller he doesn't need to reduce his price. Offer him *full* price for his property along with little or no cash down. The down payment, in his mind, can become the extra amount he's receiving for his property.

B. "Low cash down" ads

Offer the seller *less* cash down but increase the purchase price slightly. The markup on the price is a way of motivating him to accept less now in exchange for more later.

Example: Seller asks $5,000 down on a $100,000 house.

You offer him $102,000—if he'll accept only $1,000 down.

So you're paying $2,000 too much? Listen, when you've held that property for ten or fifteen years and collected more than $100,000 from it, you won't care that you paid 2 percent more than the seller asked.

9. Existing Paper for a Down Payment

If you've sold a property and hold mortgages on it, you have three problems:

A. Your value is tied to dollars which are in a depreciating asset.

B. The mortgage payments to you are strung out over a period of years with even cheaper dollars.

C. You're paying ordinary income tax on the interest earned.

Solution to all three problems: Offer your mortgages for down payments. Insist that they count for their full value. This is a key point. You'll probably hear a few no's before you get the one yes you need.

You might add a little cash as a sweetener if you have it. Example:

$15,000 down payment
$12,000 mortgage on 312 Main Street
$3,000 cash

10. Current Equity as a Down Payment

If you own a piece of property and you would like to get rid of it, offer your equity in the property (paid for or not) as a down payment on some other property, adding cash as a sweetener if you have it. Then you can start all over again depreciating the new property (assuming you qualify under the new tax laws.)

However, instead of selling the old property and paying ordinary income tax, be sure to structure a 1031 tax-free exchange for the new building. (1031 is the Internal Revenue Service form number for exchanges.) There are rules that must be followed for the tax-free exchange to be allowed. Ask your CPA.

11. Buy REOs

When institutional lenders have to foreclose a loan on a property, they put it on what they call their REO (Real Estate Owned) list. They try to keep this list as short as possible.

Oh, yes, I know there are a very few lenders who are notorious for foreclosing fast and systematically reselling the properties at a profit. But most financial institutions don't want to own real estate. It looks bad on their record, since it shows that they made loans they couldn't collect. A big inventory of REOs automatically reduces the amount they can borrow from the Federal Reserve Bank. In extreme cases it may threaten their charter, because the law sets limits on how much real estate they can own.

That's why they want to get the properties off their books quickly. But they can't go out in the marketplace and peddle them openly, since this would be undignified and bad for public relations. So if you walk in and show interest in buying, they may forget their usual skittishness about nothing-down transactions and let you buy on surprisingly favorable terms.

Call local banks and S & Ls and ask to talk to the real-estate officer. Ask him what he has in REOs right now. Sit down nose to nose and get acquainted. If you don't like what he has now, ask him to call you when something comes in.

12. Borrow on Your Life Insurance

Many of you reading this book have cash values of thousands of dollars in your life-insurance policies. You're letting the life-insurance company invest this cash and get rich on it. Why not use it to make yourself wealthy instead? Borrow out your cash value (at a very low interest rate) and invest it in real estate. That's where the insurance companies invest.

Note: For you young couples just getting started, check with your parents. They may have a cash-value policy. Let them borrow the money, you borrow it from them, and pay them perhaps 2 percent more than they will be paying the insurance company. You could give them a second or third mortgage on the property you're buying.

13. Take Partners

It's often said that the more money a man makes, the less time he has for other things. There is a lot of truth in this. Salaries of $100,000 generally come with 70-hour work weeks. But have you ever met a person who couldn't use some extra cash (especially with the new tax rates, where he gets to keep most of it). What better way is there for him to increase his income than from the profits of real-estate transactions that don't involve his time (70 hours per week is enough).

Who does have time? You do.

You can use your spare ten hours a week to find properties that you and your newfound partner can buy. Look at the benefits to you: Suddenly you represent a buyer with a strong financial statement and credit rating (your partner). With his money, you can handle both the small down payment (if any) and any negative cash flow. And remember the main benefits that accrue to him. He gets more income, keeps more of it (low tax rates), and enjoys profits without wasting time.

14. Borrow from Credit Unions

Many of you reading this book belong to credit unions. They are good sources of loans for down payments.

Remember, if you borrow the down payment from another source, it is still a "no down payment" purchase for you. Credit-union loans usually have lower interest rates than bank loans.

Credit unions are also good sources of Title One loans. These are federally insured loans used to fix up property. You can borrow up to $2,500 with *no* lien on your property.

15. Paper the Broker

The real-estate broker's commission of 5 to 7 percent is sometimes a stumbling block to a transaction. Many properties are listed for 10 percent down. Do you know what the 10 percent is for? Broker's commission and closing costs. Surprisingly often, a broker would rather wait for his commission than lose a sale. So offer him a note for it. If you can borrow from the broker and creatively eliminate closing costs (see next technique for help), then you can buy with none of your own cash.

16. Use Tenants' Money as a Down Payment

Rents are paid in advance—but payments on a loan are made after using the money for a month.

You can use this knowledge to generate down payments.

When negotiating a transaction, arrange that the final papers will be signed (that is, the "closing" will take place) on the first or second of the month. That's when you'll become the new owner.

Since the rents are paid forward, you will get credit for them. A ten-unit building renting at $400 per unit equals $4,000 in your bank account. There's your built-in down payment!

Deposits belong to the tenants. The landlord holds them. Since you are the new landlord, the old landlord gives the deposits to you for safekeeping. If the deposit on the above ten-unit building was $200 per unit, you receive ten times $200, or $2,000, in deposits.

In this example, the right closing date puts $6,000 ($4,000 in rents plus $2,000 in deposits) at your command for a down payment.

As a buyer, then, plan your closing for the first or second of the month.

17. Create Paper

This is a magically cheap way to borrow money. It's simply creating your own mortgage.

Blank promissory notes and mortgage forms are for sale at any office-supply store. Get some and fill them in to suit your needs. Offer your equity in your home or other property as a down payment by writing a mortgage on the property and handing it over in lieu of cash.

The *terms* are negotiable. Ask for a low interest rate and a low repayment schedule with your initial offer, and negotiate from there.

18. Use Your Land

How about that piece of land you bought in Nowhere Estates? You've already paid for it or the loan balance is small. Fine. Offer the land as a down payment on a piece of income property. Add a little cash if you have it.

Don't let a few refusals discourage you. One acceptance is all you need. But be sure to structure a tax-free exchange—your land for the seller's house. Your CPA can help you with this.

19. Buy with Credit Cards

For quick closes when you locate a good buy, you'll need a credit line of instant cash. Start now to set it up. You can do this by acquiring an assortment of different credit cards. You can have as many different Master Card or VISA accounts as you want. Even if you already have one or two, get more—but get them all at the same time, to avoid flak from the credit bureau.

The point is, each card entitles you to a certain amount of credit. If the credit limit on each card is $500, ten cards give you an instant $5,000 line of credit.

Here's how you get multiple cards. First go down to TRW, a national credit reporting company (look in the Yellow Pages under Credit Reporting Agencies), and buy a copy of its credit report on you. There's almost certainly one in its files. Make photocopies of the report. Send a copy along with each of your applications for a credit card. Why do it this way? Because otherwise the card issuers would ask the credit bureau for a report on you. The bureau records all credit checks, including the names of the inquirers. If a lot of inquiries about you hit the bureau at the same time, alarm bells would ring. But there'll be no inquiries, since the lenders already have the credit report, thoughtfully provided by you. None of those lenders will see each other's names on the report, since you got it before applying.

All this may be a bother, but it is perfectly legal and sooner or later you'll be glad you went to the trouble. A day will come when a fast $3,000 or $4,000 in cash can make you $20,000. Don't miss it!

20. Buy Government-Owned Homes

Thousands of home loans are insured by the Veterans Administration (VA), the Federal Housing Administration (FHA), and various other agencies of the Department of Housing and Urban Development (HUD). If one of these loans goes sour, the government agency forecloses, pays off the lender and tries to sell the home. These agencies have countless foreclosed properties they would love to get off their books. You can step up and buy some in nothing down transactions (Chapter 10 will tell you more about these agencies).

To get information about properties, phone the agencies and ask, "How can I be put on a list to be notified about foreclosures for sale?" You can call the VA's information office in Washington at (202)389-2443. FHA is part of HUD and you can call HUD's public affairs offices at (202)755-6980 or (202)755-6420.

You may also be able to get information you need locally. Federal installations are listed alphabetically in the phone book under U.S. Government, which you'll usually find on page 1. Look up the number of the Federal Information Center nearest you. FIC is a government agency "providing a single point for the public to address questions about federal agencies and programs. Callers receive the desired information or are told how to contact the office that can assist them." If you live near one of the bigger cities, its FIC office may help you get data about local foreclosures from a mini-headquarters of VA, FHA or HUD in that city.

21. Offer the Seller a Bonus for Paying Closing Costs

"Mr. Seller, I'm a little short on the $1,600 for closing costs. How about your paying them, if I add $2,000 to the second mortgage you'll be carrying?"

22. Split Funding

Suppose a seller wants one-fifth down and he won't budge. You can suggest, "Okay, I'll pay one-fifth down if you take half of the amount now, half a year from now."

That means a 10 percent down payment now. Try to whittle it way down by using techniques 15, 16 and 21.

Then you have a year to find a partner and sell him half the building for enough cash to cover the remaining 10 percent down payment.

This is a real money-cranker if you are buying the building below market for a quick turnover at market. If the rents are below market, raise them. Then get a new appraisal, which will be higher. Your new partner will pay you half of the higher appraised value.

In Chapter 15, I'll show you a way to make extra profit on a split-funding offer just by the way you word the offer.

9

WORKING WITH LENDERS—OR, WHERE'S YOUR DOWN PAYMENT?

YOU PROBABLY REMEMBER THE OLD JOKE ABOUT THE banker's glass eye—it's the one with the warmth of human kindness in it. And there was Robert Frost's definition of a bank as "a place where they lend you an umbrella in fair weather and ask for it back again when it begins to rain."

As someone else said, banks are not in the business of lending money, they are in the business of *making* money. My own pet axiom along this line is, "Banks never lend money to people who need money. Banks lend money to people who don't need money."

In spite of all this, your real-estate investing will probably have to make use of banks and similar institutions such as savings and loan associations. "Banks are where the money is," Willie Sutton, the noted bank robber, said in explaining why he favored them.

So let's look at them. The more you understand about institutional lenders, the easier you can borrow money.

This chapter will show you various smart moves you can make in dealing with them, and I hope it will help you get over any fear of banks and bankers you may feel.

Good and Bad Times to Borrow

It pays to shop around when you need a real-estate loan from a lending institution. I'm always amazed how

98

few borrowers do this. Studies have shown, *The Wall Street Journal* says, that only one in three home buyers asks more than one lender about mortgage terms and types.

In your own shopping, here are factors to keep in mind.

When a bank is new and/or small, that's a good time to approach it for loans. It is looking for customers. "The only way a bank is going to grow is by making loans," Charles Agemian often said. He is the man who left New York's huge Chase Manhattan Bank and moved across the river to become chairman of Garden State National Bank, which then had about $120 million in assets. Four years later its assets were more than $500 million.

You might consider opening an account, long before you need to borrow, in any new bank or small bank near you. Get acquainted there. Ask the bank's officers for advice about this or that. See if you can become friendly with the president or the chief loan officer. Obviously this is easier to do in a bank that's trying to expand and reaching out for new customers. If you mention that you expect to acquire quite a few properties—hand out your DBA cards—you'll get a big handshake and maybe an invitation to lunch.

By contrast, if a bank is old and sleepy, or just fat and happy, even knowing the president may not help much. Believe it or not, there are some banks where the president can't make a loan over nine hundred dollars without going to a loan committee for authorization.

If there's only one bank or S & L in your community, it's bad news for borrowers. No competition means no ambition. Better get in your car and drive to wherever there's brisk rivalry.

A good time to borrow is when banks are expanding their business. It happened during the 1960s and may be happening near you right now, with the big switch to electronic teller machines and the rush into new fields like interstate banking. "Consumer lending and home mortgage lending have been growing," according to *Value Line's* national survey of the bank industry at the end of 1983.

Now and then a bank tries to brighten up its reputation by putting out stacks of publicity about its loans to minorities, veterans, small businesses and other fairly risky but deserving groups. If you're buying from (or selling to) someone in one of these groups, you'll get a friendly hearing at the bank.

Some of the worst times to borrow are when:

1. there's a recession;

2. there's trouble in the parent bank because of bad loans or other losses;

3. interest rates are high;

4. a bank's deposits are low and it is trying to nurse them along by cutting down on loans. Lenders often raise interest rates instead of admitting they are out of money.

Nothing Down? Bankers Frown

But let's face one fact. Whether the timing is good or bad, you won't be greeted warmly if lending establishments know you want to buy real estate with little or no down payment. It goes against their code. They want you to have plenty of your own money or collateral tied up in the transaction.

Therefore they give borrowers a loan application which is designed to screen out nothing-down buyers. It contains two killer questions:

A: "Is there any secondary financing on this property?" (This is to prevent the seller from carrying back all of his equity in the form of a secondary mortgage.)

B: "What is the source of your down payment?" (This is to assure the lender you have put something down.)

But cheer up. The above doesn't mean you can't

make a nothing down purchase with financing from a bank or an S & L. It just means you must use imaginative tactics. This whole book is supposed to stimulate your imagination, or at least to start you out with an armful of unusual techniques.

Four Ways to Solve the Problem

Here are four basic solutions to the problem. Let's take them one by one and see how they get you past the two tough questions.

Solution 1: Have the seller take your unsecured personal note.

This works best with friends, relatives or acquaintances; it usually runs into resistance with strangers. However, don't assume all strangers will refuse. Always ask. There are only two answers, and one is great. If you get it, you can answer the bank's questions as follows:

Question A (any secondary financing): your answer is "No."

Question B (source of your down payment): "Notes and/or other valuable considerations to be delivered at the time of closing."

Solution 2: Transfer the mortgage. In other words, use another piece of property as collateral for the second mortgage. You actually put the mortgage carried back by the seller on another piece of property. Then your answers are:

Question A: "No."

Question B: "Equity and/or mortgages on other property to be delivered at time of closing."

Solution 3: Buy on a contract (That is, a "Contract for Deed" or "Contract of Sale.")

At this point you may want to skip ahead to Chapter 14 where I talk about selling property on a contract. The basic idea is that the title doesn't change hands until the date fixed by contract. Instead of buying the house, you promise in writing that you'll buy it at the future date. The contract for deed, since title does not pass, does not put the lender in a position where he can call the loan in most states. (Note: there are a few states like Colorado, where adverse court decisions prevent sale on a contract without the loan being called. Before starting to buy check with a real-estate attorney about the current situation in your state.)

There are two special cases where you can give the seller all cash in a short period of time and still buy with none of your money. Offer to buy on a contract with a very short due date, say six to twelve months. In other words, the seller would get his price, all cash, when the contract comes due in that six-to-twelve-month period. This would work where two conditions exist.

1. You can buy the building at 80 percent or below of appraised value, which will let you get a loan from a lender for enough to cash out the seller with the lender's money.

2. You had a way to raise the building's value quickly, such as making cosmetic improvements and boosting the rent substantially. The new value of the property (after the rent is raised) must be enough so that the new loan cashes out the seller.

Solution 4: Have the seller refinance.

Some lifelong home owners aren't familiar with the idea of refinancing and hate the thought of borrowing. You may need to explain everything to them in completely nontechnical terms. You say something like this:

"Since I'm not putting any cash down, Mr. Seller, it's going to be difficult for me to get the new loan. However, it would be easy for you to get the new loan since you would be refinancing a property you already own and they wouldn't ask for a down payment. Sure the interest will be higher, but that's my problem, not yours. I'm going to take over the payment and I'll put that in our written agreement."

For the seller's protection, he does need your contract to purchase the property and assume the bank loan. After the loan is in place, you take it over, and have the seller take back a second mortgage for the rest of his equity.

Under this method, no sale is taking place at the time of the loan, just a refinance. So Questions A (secondary financing on property) and B (source of down payment) have no meaning.

How to Get a High Appraisal

How much a bank will lend depends on the property's value as established by an appraisal. Banks use only M.A.I. (Member Appraisers Institute) appraisers. In fact, they tend to use the more conservative M.A.I.s. Knowing all this, you can take advantage of it.

Call the bank's loan department (anonymously). Tell them, "I want to get a property appraised by a good M.A.I. Which ones do you use?"

When you get the answer, hire one of those appraisers. He now works for you, not the bank.

Tell him you want the highest appraisal he can give you and still sleep nights. This will put your property valuation at the higher end of the scale.

Now you're ready to ask the money temple for a loan. The loan officer will say, "We'll have to get the property appraised."

You will say, "I just did."

He will say, "That's nice, but I'm sorry, the appraiser has to be one of ours."

You say, "Who are they?" He will tell you.

Then you say, "What a coincidence! I used the appraiser you just mentioned."

The banker will mutter, "We don't normally do it this way," but he can't very well reject the appraisal. Banks don't normally do it your way because they lose the extra dollars they would add on top of the normal cost for the appraisal. Since their way includes making you pay for the appraisal, you haven't spent any money you wouldn't spend anyway. But you get a larger loan because the appraised value is higher.

Getting Ready to Talk

In addition to the appraisal, there are other preparations you would make before talking with a banker.

First fill out a complete, up-to-date financial statement. Banks like to study this. Failure to provide one is a major reason for delays or turndowns on a loan.

I always add a touch of my own that draws pleased murmurs from bankers: I include a separate sheet of all my current real-estate loans *including* addresses and phone numbers of the lenders, for easy contact by the bank. That simple addition has brought me statements from many bankers like, "This is the most complete application form I've ever seen."

In addition to your financial statement, banks often want you to fill out a questionnaire with information about your age, marital status and other matters that might seem to be none of their business. They're evaluating your personal creditworthiness, and they have their own private point scale for rating your answers. If you have to fill out one of these, be sure to answer every question. An unanswered question will count against you more than a borderline answer. (In the next chapter I'll give you a load of advice about establishing credit.)

One more thing to do before talking with a banker: Make sure your plan for repaying the loan is clear in your mind. You'll need to explain it clearly to him. You want to be able to say, early in the conversation, "The nice thing about this loan is the ease with which we can repay it"—music to a banker's ears. Repayment is all-important to bankers.

Secrets of Successful Conversation

"This is a good loan and I wanted to bring it to you first" is a remark that has a good effect on money men. It implies that you're doing them a favor because other banks will jump at this loan.

When a banker asks a question, always try to answer with a question. For example, when he says, "How much do you want to borrow?" you ask, "How much will you lend me?" Maybe you'd settle for $2,000 but if he's willing to lend $5,000, why take less? Remember, if you mention a specific sum, that's the most you'll get. Let the banker name the amount, then try to negotiate him upward if necessary.

Never use the words "I need" when talking to a banker. If he were a dog his ears would perk up at those words. He never lends to needy people. Regardless of what you say from that point on, or how good your application is, you're a goner. He'll tell you something like "Your credit looks good, and I wish we could accommodate you, but we don't make this type of loan." You'll never hear the real reason you were brushed off.

To avoid the bad vibes of "I need," substitute these much better words: "I could use . . ." or "That amount would handle it."

A Way to Change No to Yes

Let's say you want a $10,000 loan on a property in order to put a transaction together. The S & L secretly decides the neighborhood isn't right, or your financial statement looks shaky, or for some other reason doesn't want to lend on the property. (Maybe it's just that the S & L isn't flush with money.) Here's one strategy that will turn the loan officer into a positive thinker.

Just say to him, "If I put $10,000 into your bank in a certificate of deposit, will you make the loan?"

In many cases there'll be a prompt yes. For every dollar on deposit, the S & L can lend out many dollars. So a $10,000 CD is a princely gift.

Probably you're thinking, "Hey, wait. I'm not going to put $10,000 in their vault to find a $10,000 loan." Of course you're not. This is a book about other people's money, right?

When the lender says yes, you say, "Fine, I'll be back in a few days." Then you put an ad in the paper. It goes in the classified column headed "Money Wanted." The ad should read:

WILL PAY TWO POINTS TO A PERSON
WILLING TO MOVE MONEY

Believe me, your phone will ring. People with money want to rent it out somewhere. Why shouldn't they move it out of their S & L and into yours and earn an extra 2 percent in cash for their trouble?

What does this cost you? Well, 2 percent of $10,000 (two points) is $200. So your extra expense of $200 wins you a yes instead of no on your loan, and you make all the profit on your property.

The important fact to understand is that the $10,000 deposit is *not* collateral for your loan, so the investor is not put at any risk. The Federal Deposit Insurance Corporation still insures his money at your S & L, just as in the other one. The deposit is only a sweetener that induces the S & L to grant your loan.

Bankers Love These Loans

Once you become a property owner, certain types of loan are easy to get. One is a home-improvement loan. This is good for unexpected major repairs—a new roof or furnace, for example. Repayment terms are easy.

Others are called Title One loans. These are government-insured loans. Since they're insured, there isn't much risk to the bank, and it charges a lower rate. Some banks don't make them. Others make them but don't advertise them. To find out, open the Yellow Pages and call loan officers.

Title One loans are easier to find in loose money markets, much harder when money is tight. These loans are made to fix up property. If the loan is $2,500 or less, there's no lien on your property.

Games Bankers Play

Even when everything looks fine and a banker is making happy sounds and your loan is going through, watch yourself. Bankers play little games to pry an extra ¼ or ½ percent out of borrowers.

If you ask about the interest rate beforehand, a banker may say something like "That depends," or "We can work that out a little later." If he sees you're up against a deadline to complete a transaction, he'll stall, hoping that the time pressure will soften your resistance. He will want to nail down the repayment schedule, collateral and everything else, then set the interest rate when you have no more room or time to negotiate.

If possible, he won't mention the rate at all but will just fill it in on the note. He'll compare it with finance-company rates, second-mortgage rates and the cost of venture capital.

At the last possible moment, he'll say, "Since you need the money today, let's write it up at X percent. Then we can talk later about changing it." He hopes you'll never bring it up again. If you do, guess how much chance you have of getting it changed.

If none of his strategies work, he may say flatly, "The rate for this type of loan is so-and-so." That's seldom true. It's negotiable. Rather than let the loan go to a competitor, he may lower the rate if he knows you're shopping around. So try to allow yourself plenty of time for comparison shopping, even after the loan seems to be certain.

It's always a good idea to pop the question about

interest rather early. Never suggest any particular rate. When he mentions a figure, be ready to look shocked, no matter what it is. He may be just feeling you out. As I say, if he wants to make the loan, he'll dicker.

Don't take his word for anything. If he agrees to some special concession, make sure it's in writing—or you may not have it at all. Read all the printed forms and documents. Ask him to explain anything you don't understand.

Look Out for the Catch Clauses

A good attorney can be invaluable in handling a bank loan document. Banks have standard forms that bind you tightly and stack everything in their favor. Some of their clauses can be crossed out, and the loan will still be made. A good attorney will know what is negotiable and what isn't.

The two worst traps to look out for are a prepayment clause and a nonassumable clause.

The prepayment clause is an effort to make sure you'll pay all the interest, which may add up to several times the principal. For example, on a $65,000 loan at 13.25 percent for 30 years, the interest ($198,000) is three times the principal. This clause will force you to pay a cash penalty to the bank if you sell the property. If you can't negotiate it out, insist that the amount of the penalty is to be reduced with time. Say the prepayment penalty goes down one fifth per year, so after five years there is no penalty.

The nonassumable clause (often called a "Due on Sale" clause) allows the lender to declare your loan due and payable in full immediately if you sell the property or transfer title.

Most conventional lenders now make this a standard clause, and won't take it out. A few of them allow *one* assumption, which lets *you* sell but traps the person you sell to.

When borrowing from a private lender, avoid this clause. If you must deal with a bank or an S & L, there are some possible defenses, depending on how its particular clause is written and what the laws in your state cover. Ask your attorney about the following strategies.

Avoiding the "Nonassumable" Trap

1. Contract of Sale. I mentioned this earlier in the chapter, and will give more detail about it in Chapter 14. Instead of buying the property, you are contracting to buy it at a future date. The title won't transfer until that date. This arrangement may be called a contract for deed, or some other name, in your state. In many states, lenders aren't trying to call the loan as long as the borrower retains title, even though he is committed to sell.

2. Let the seller keep a 1 percent interest in the home he is selling. This may work if the Due on Sale clause doesn't say "or part." The house isn't being sold, only part of it (99 percent).

3. See if the title to the property is in the name of a corporation or partnership, as it often is in real estate. If you can buy the corporation or the partnership, you get the property but the title stays in the same name, so the Due on Sale clause isn't triggered.

4. Make your buyer a lender. Let's say he gives you cash for your equity, and in return you give him a second mortgage on your house equal to that amount. You then have problems making payments. You may deed it back to him after falling behind on your payments. So now, as a lender, he can apply to the first mortgage holder to assume their mortgage at the current rate. This often works because lenders have a gentlemen's agreement: They don't foreclose on other lenders. No actual foreclosure takes place. And there is no reporting to the credit bureau. Form a DBA (see Index). Is his name Wilson? He becomes Wilson Mortgage Company. Get stationery printed and write on his letterhead that he has

been given a deed in lieu of foreclosure, and he would like to assume the loan at current rates until such time as he disposes of the property.

Beating the Points

Another expensive clause in a loan document requires you to pay "points."

Points are a legal gimmick to collect more interest without raising the interest rate on the loan. They were invented in order to get around usury laws in the individual states. "Usury" is a word you never hear in lenders' offices. It means "extortionate or exorbitant interest," according to one definition. That's the kind of interest charged by illegal loan sharks. To avoid being classed with such people, banks charge points instead.

A point is 1 percent of the loan, paid in advance. One point on a $50,000 loan would be $500, and on a $100,000 loan it's a cool grand.

Always remember: points are negotiable. The more money lying idle in the lender's vaults, the more negotiable the points are. Be sure you negotiate.

If a lender tells you, "We charge two points," you should say, "No, I wouldn't want to pay that." Then shut up. Let him be the next to talk. You may hear one and a half points, or one point. Never accept the first number. Always try for a lower one. Sometimes you'll win, sometimes not. But you'll never win if you don't try.

Balloons Aren't So Bad

A balloon payment in a mortgage is just about what it sounds like: a big payment after a series of small ones. To say this another way, part of the mortgage (usually all or most of the principal) is due in a lump sum after a number of equal monthly payments.

Thinking about that big sum can be scary if you don't see the money in view to make the payment. But don't be afraid. Properly used, a balloon is a handy tool to make money in real estate. Here are two uses:

1. It can induce a seller to carry back a mortgage on his property. It shows him that he won't have to wait a long time for his money, as he might if he accepted an amortized mortgage.

2. It can keep your monthly debt payments low (less than amortized) so the rent from tenants will put you in the black each month.

The big question about balloon payments is, *When* will the balloon come due? One or two years is too soon. Always avoid short fuses.

I like ten-year balloon payments. In any ten-year span a property should double or better, and the balloon will be easy to handle. The shortest I want to accept is five years. For less than that I'll want some serious concessions from the seller.

When a balloon due date is approaching, you'll have plenty of options. You can sell, refinance, take a second mortgage. Read Chapter 12 and see all the things you can do. Just make sure you start planning in plenty of time.

Now let's consider down payments again from a different angle. At the beginning of this chapter I showed you how to get around the banks' dislike of nothing down transactions. But you also should realize that you may be able to make a down payment to the seller after all.

Six Ways to Make a Down Payment

To start with, your own home offers you three possible sources of money for a down payment:

1. Refinance to pull cash out in exchange for equity. Wait for a time when credit is easy and interest rates are low.

2. Take a second mortgage. Again, wait for a loose money market.

3. Offer a note. Create your own promissory note and mortgage on your home. Offer it for a down payment (look back at Chapter 8). Don't forget to propose *low* payments on your note.

Due to the Texas homestead law, the above three strategies can't be used there—unless the law has been repealed by the time you read this. Anyhow, there are three other possibilities not involving your home:

4. Offer anything for a down payment. And I do mean anything, or almost anything.

You may own a lot of things that someone would accept as a down payment. Get a pencil and paper and make an inventory of everything you own.

Go down the list to see what you could part with, happily, or even reluctantly, in order to become financially independent.

You might add a little cash as a sweetener if you have it. Also, keep in mind that an item doesn't have to be totally paid off. Here are just a few ideas. Add your own:

a) autos
b) airplanes
c) boats
d) computers
e) furniture
f) jewelry
g) lots
h) motor homes
i) raw land in the boon-docks
j) tools
k) your pet giraffe

5. Sweat equity as a down payment. Let's say you find a property that does need fixing up, and you happen to be a good handyman. Offer no down payment and include in your agreement "Buyer agrees, as a condition of purchase, to make the following repairs within 30 days." Include a detailed list of repairs on your offer form.

This plants the thought in the seller's mind that if he ever has to take the property back, it will be worth a lot more because of the repairs you made. The cost of the repairs should be mostly labor (your labor).

6. Your labor as a down payment. This sounds like number 5 but it isn't. I mean a different kind of labor now.

You work at a job or business and you have an area of expertise, be it a hobby or a trade or a profession. It doesn't matter whether you are a lawyer, doctor, plumber, carpenter, bricklayer or whatever. Offer perhaps twenty hours of your services in barter as a substitute for cash. If the seller has a need for your expertise at the time, he may jump at your offer.

Get the idea? Start writing offers, using any of the above as your proposed down payment. Remember, it only takes one yes among all those no's. Every time you hear a yes, you've bought a property without cash!

10

NO CREDIT?
WHAT TO DO

PROBABLY YOU'VE HEARD OVER AND OVER, "YOU can't buy real estate without good credit." Bunk!

I found out early that I could buy property without money and without credit. Anyone else can do what I did.

I was thirty-eight years old, had been a renter all my life and didn't have a good credit rating. My wife and I got what seemed like a crazy idea at first: We ought to invest in real estate. Everybody told us immediately that we couldn't. But we were stubborn. We kept circulating, telling everyone we met, "We want to buy a home."

We quickly found a man who had to sell one. He had to leave the state in two weeks, and he had to sell that house before he left. We sat down with him and worked it out. He would sell for a very small down payment and carry back the financing. In short, he gave us the credit we needed. We had discovered motivated sellers.

Take Credit for Yourself

We thought, "If there is one seller like this out here, there must be more."

We were right. We found many more. We just kept buying as fast as we could—borrowing from sellers, not from banks. The first million dollars I borrowed, I didn't fill out one loan application, and no one verified my income or checked my credit. There isn't one person reading this book who can't do the same thing.

However, I don't mean to imply that buying without credit is always the best way. Although good credit isn't a requirement for buying real estate, it is a major benefit. Later in this chapter I'll show you how to establish good credit in a few weeks.

But for the moment, let's say you're in my original position. You want to start investing in real estate now. You're cash poor and your credit rating is low or nonexistent. How do you get started?

Of course, you stay away from conventional lenders like banks and S & Ls. You can go out and negotiate with motivated sellers, as I did. I've already shown you more than two dozen kinds of offers you can make to these sellers. But I haven't said much about what may be the easiest of all arrangements for buying property without credit: get Uncle Sam to stand behind you.

A Guarantee from the Government

You see, mortgages are different from other loans. Property is the security for a mortgage loan. So the quality of the property is much more important to lenders than many facts about the borrower's character, wealth, health or anything else. If the land and the building are good, the lender can always take them back in case of default, so the net worth of the borrower can be much less than if it were a signature loan. The main requirement of a lender is a good credit rating. A good credit rating not only indicates an *ability* to repay, but also a *willingness* to repay. Although the building is the collateral, the lender wants reasonable assurance he won't have to take the property back. He looks for a track record indicating that the buyer has paid his bills in the past.

About fifty years ago the government got into the act

of making it easier and a lot less risky to own real estate. They made the lender much more motivated to make a loan by eliminating the need for the lender to take back the property in case of default. Now where does the U.S. Government fit into your investment program? To understand this, it helps to know a bit of history.

Until 1934, anyone who mortgaged his house or farm was in a terribly dangerous position. A mortgage in those days was usually an interest-only loan with a fixed term. It had to be paid off or renewed at the end of the term. If it fell due when economic conditions were bad, the lender would probably refuse to renew. In most cases that meant that the borrower lost his property, because he couldn't find anyone else to borrow from and he couldn't pay off the mortgage. Thousands of people did become homeless that way after the Great Depression in 1929.

In foreclosing, the lenders were just using good business judgment. The value of houses and farms can deteriorate in a depression. Between 1929 and 1933, property values shrank so much (there was deflation in those years, not inflation) that a lender was foolish to renew a mortgage unless the borrower could pay off a big part of the loan. Very few borrowers could do this. Unemployment was at record levels, and farm crops weren't selling.

But in 1934 the New Dealers and Congress came up with a solution: the self-amortizing mortgage plus a government guarantee that the mortgage would eventually be paid. The Federal Housing Administration (FHA) was set up to insure mortgage loans made by private banks on new and older homes, and on rental and cooperative projects. FHA made no loans itself but merely underwrote the financing arrangements between bank and borrower.

The plan didn't catch on quickly. Most bankers were sure the Supreme Court would declare the whole scheme unconstitutional. Besides, the legislation didn't put any money in their pockets, or even in the pockets of their friends, the builders. They disliked the "interference" of FHA, its appraisers and its paperwork.

On the other hand, FHA mortgages did offer people a chance to own their own homes at a cost not much higher than rent. The monthly mortgage payments were big enough to cover both interest charges (very low in those times) and the complete repayment of the loan over the life of the mortgage. The day when the mortgage ended was a day of celebration, instead of despair and doom as it usually had been in the past.

Progressive bankers in the West saw the possibilities and began lending millions with FHA backing. The revolution gradually spread to even the stodgiest financial institutions.

Credit, Credit Everywhere

FHA's benefit to the banks was that its nationwide network of appraisers gave mortgage holders protection when lending on properties they didn't know and couldn't investigate. Generally the builder of a house, not the buyer or borrower, had to qualify for FHA insurance, so these mortgages were safer and more negotiable. This made them more attractive to lenders and less expensive for both lender and borrower.

FHA financing totaled only $533 million in 1936 but grew to $7 billion by 1970. Today about 15 percent of all mortgage loans on private dwellings are FHA insured. Foreclosures are rare. But when one happens, FHA pays off the lender and then tries to sell the property at a fair market price. (Back in Chapter 8 we saw how to buy these foreclosed houses.)

Do you see what FHA insurance means to you as an investor?

It means that if you buy from someone whose property has an FHA mortgage on it, you can take over the low payments on that mortgage and the bank won't worry—FHA will pay if you don't. In most cases, just signing your name on a loan document enables you to assume a debt of tens of thousands of dollars with no credit check. There are thousands of these loans all around the country, just waiting to help credit-poor investors buy homes.

Another government-financing vehicle you should know about is the Veterans Administration.

The VA was set up in 1944 under the Servicemen's Readjustment Act, commonly known as the GI Bill of Rights. Since 1945 it has guaranteed more than $75 billion in loans (including low-interest home loans) to veterans of World War II, the Korean War and the Vietnam War.

Like the FHA, the VA doesn't lend money—it just insures. It covers the first half of any losses a bank might suffer on a mortgage loan to a veteran, up to a certain maximum per house. This protects lenders against all but the worst stupidity, even on loans for houses bought with no down payment at all. (In 1951 the rules were changed to require down payments on VA mortgages, and higher down payments on FHA mortgages. But the interest rates are still low, so you get a bargain when you assume one.)

Banks and S & Ls are still making FHA and VA home loans. Since the loans are foolproof, lenders don't normally run credit checks on a person assuming one. So never let anyone tell you that you must establish credit to buy property. You can always buy from people whose mortgages are insured by Uncle Sam. If they're motivated to sell, they'll take your note and let you take over their payments.

How do you find these people? By looking in your newspaper's classified ads under "Real Estate For Sale." Pick out ads with headlines like these:

VA

FHA

NO CREDIT CHECK

BUY WITHOUT CREDIT

Many FHA and VA bargains aren't advertised. Some are listed through real-estate brokers, but don't expect the broker or salesman to alert you to them. Ask to be shown the homes in your price range or neighborhood with existing FHA or VA loans. You'll be amazed at how many there are, in all but the very expensive neighborhoods.

Promise Now, Buy Later

In Chapter 9 I mentioned a financing vehicle called a contract of sale, or contract for deed (some states have various other names for it). You'll find more about it in Chapter 14. But it ought to be mentioned here too, because it belongs on any list of the easiest ways to buy without credit.

You sign a contract committing you to buy the property on an agreed future date. The seller retains title until then. You make payments for the stipulated period, after which you receive the deed. Since you aren't assuming a loan, there is no real requirement for a credit check (in a few cases the seller may insist).

But be cautious. Since you are not receiving title to the property, some bad things could happen to you:

1. The seller might get into financial difficulties. A court judgment against him, or a bankruptcy, could produce liens against your title.

2. The seller might die. Settling his estate might take years, especially if there were a bunch of creditors or a pending lawsuit. Something like this could tie up your title for a long time.

3. The seller might be unscrupulous enough to sell the property to someone else, in violation of his contract with you. Then you might have to sue for breach of contract, and again the title could be clouded.

How can you protect yourself against these dangers? Here are some suggestions.

Record the contract. This prevents the seller from selling the piece of property more than once.

At the time you negotiate the contract, put in a clause that the seller will place a signed deed to the property in a neutral depository such as an escrow company, bank or attorney's office.

The buyer (you) should have the right to take possession of the deed and record it if the seller dies, or if you've made payments for a specified period of time. (Try for one to three years.)

Try to take title if it is feasible to do so. Assume the first mortgage if the interest rate isn't too high. Let the owner carry a second mortgage. Or buy on a wraparound mortgage. (Check with several local brokers to see if lenders can demand full payment in your state if a wraparound mortgage is placed over the existing mortgages.)

Easy Ways to Establish Credit

So you have no credit? Or your credit rating is fair to poor?

Neither of these handicaps needs to slow you down for more than a few weeks. They are definitely curable.

If you have no credit, the following technique will establish credit. If you have weak or bad credit, the same technique will put a good credit performance record in front of the bad one.

The best credit, of course, is bank credit. You need it in order to borrow from banks, and it helps mightily in borrowing from other lenders. So go get yourself bank credit. Here's how.

If you haven't joined your local apartment owners'

association, do it. At your next meeting, ask them *which* banks are kindest to real-estate investors. That's important because you'll be borrowing a *lot* of money from them later on.

Go out tomorrow to three of those banks and set up a savings account at each. For this example, we'll say you put a thousand dollars in each account. If you don't have three thousand dollars, then put several hundred in each.

Now wait a few business days. It takes that long for the bank's computers to get organized (some of them never get organized).

Next, go back to each bank and ask the loan officer for a thousand-dollar loan (or several hundred if that's what you put in). Tell the loan officer you want to pledge your savings account as collateral. Do bankers like this kind of loan? They love it because the repayment money is already locked in their vaults. It's what they call a "fully secured" loan.

Of course they may think you're a little strange. "What are you going to do with the money?" is a question they often ask. Your answer is that you're building credit.

It's important that the loan be for six months or longer so it will go on your credit report. But don't wait six months to repay it. After one week, make an installment payment on all three loans. After a second week, make another installment payment on them.

From then on, make normal monthly payments. But after four or five weeks, call up the bank's collection department and ask him/her to report your loan to the local credit bureau. (They would probably do this anyway later on, but you can speed up the process.)

Now you'll have great current credit in any major city in this country. Whenever you fill out a credit application, list Bank A, Bank B, and Bank C as your credit references (notice they all ask for three credit references).

With these references, you can apply for one or more

of the national credit cards like VISA or American Express and probably be accepted. Credit cards are useful in real estate, as I'll show you in a minute.

Naturally lenders investigate borrowers. They'd go broke if they didn't. In addition to phoning your credit references, they'll also ask the credit bureau about you.

Credit bureaus exist in every city and keep files on borrowers—how fast they pay their bills, how often they get into trouble, how much they make, how often they change jobs, and so on. Any bad or good information stays on your record for seven years. If you declare bankruptcy, this fact stays on your record for ten years.

But the newest information takes priority and carries most weight. Your good record with the three banks should be enough to satisfy most lenders, especially when the current loan is secured against real estate.

Even if you're moving around, your credit report will follow you. Retail Credit Company and Credit Data Company (now a subsidiary of the big conglomerate corporation TRW) has computerized its files nationwide, and it makes these available to local bureaus or lenders.

If there's any doubt about your credit rating, you can go to the bureau and ask for a copy of its report on you. By law, the bureau must give it to you, although it will charge a small fee for the favor (if you have been turned down for credit in the last thirty days they must give you a copy free). You'll find the report full of confusing symbols and numbers. Ask the bureau to explain what these mean.

Other Arts of Borrowing

Instead of depositing cash in banks and borrowing against it, there are other ways to get a "fully secured" loan. If you happen to own stocks or bonds, take the certificates to a bank and offer to pledge some of these as collateral for your loan. Any institution will lend at least half the value of the securities as quoted in current stock market reports. Usually the securities will be kept in your name, so you'll still receive the dividend payments as usual.

If your car is paid for, banks will often accept the ownership certificate ("pink slip") as collateral for a loan.

A trickier method, available only if you have trusting and well-heeled friends or relatives, is known as the double-loan technique. Say you have only $3,000 but need to borrow $10,000. Deposit your $3,000 and get a passbook loan for that amount. Arrange for your friends to borrow the $10,000. Then you give them the $3,000 as interest on the $10,000 for, say, two years at 15 percent a year. At the end of the two years you should be able to pay off the loans yourself from your profits, or to refinance them if you need more time.

I went into detail on the use of credit cards in Chapter 8. If you're going to own some apartments, be sure to set up a line of credit with a bank or several banks, even if it's just several VISA cards with $500 credit on each. You want to have instant access to a few thousand dollars, no questions asked. Then, if there are sudden vacancies in your apartments, and you need cash to make the mortgage payment (or to pay for cleaning and refurbishing if needed to get apartments ready for rerenting) there's no problem.

After you've established credit at banks, make a yearly practice of asking them to increase the credit limit. You can probably get this boost with just a phone call.

Always keep in mind the underlying theme of this book: The way to build wealth through real-estate investment is to use other people's money. "Money" isn't usually coins or greenbacks. It also comes in many other forms, mostly invisible. Eighty to ninety percent of the "money" in this country doesn't exist. It hasn't been printed, minted or coined. It's electrons on bank computers. Go out and get your share of it.

11

STRUCTURING YOUR OFFER TO STAY OUT OF TROUBLE

ANY GOOD BUSINESSMAN WILL TELL YOU IT'S A TERRI-ble mistake to get too much working capital tied up in fixed assets like real estate.

You won't make that mistake. This chapter will show you how not to.

You're going to put as little as possible of your own capital into any one property, so you can keep money at work in a lot of properties instead of just one. And you're going to put at least one user (a rent-paying occupant) in each property. You'll let the users (tenants) sit there and buy all that real estate for you with their money. They, not you, will pay off your debts on the properties.

Don't be afraid of that four-letter word "debt." Debt was an ugly word in Puritan times and for centuries after. There was a debtors' prison. People were supposed to pay as they went, to live within their incomes.

Debt: Burden or Booster

Then a smart Treasury Secretary named Alexander Hamilton came along and preached, "A national debt, if it is not excessive, will be to us a national blessing."

Jefferson picked this up and pounded it home: "A public debt is a public blessing."

Investors learned the same lesson about private debts. By borrowing (using "leverage," as it's called),

124

you can make your own money bring better returns on every dollar you invest. If you were to save up to make all-cash investments you'd be scrimping all your life.

Whatever property you buy will probably have one or more mortgages on it already. So you'll take on this debt load to begin with, paying off the seller's mortgage in the same installments, usually, that he contracted for. On top of that you've got to pay him for his equity* plus a profit—but you won't pay much of this in cash. Instead, you'll give him a note, secured by your title to the house (in other words, another mortgage or trust deed), to be paid off in whichever way the two of you agree. Your payments on these various debts are called debt service.

Debt service can eat you up if you don't understand how to structure a transaction. If your monthly payments to the lenders are bigger than the rents coming in, you have net outgo instead of net income—or "negative cash flow," as financial people usually phrase it—you're taking a loss every month.

Some real-estate operators say your profit should be built in when you buy—by which they usually mean you should buy for less than the property is worth. But I always tell people, "Negative cash flow isn't a price-of-property problem, it's a knowledge problem." In other words, reducing or eliminating it just requires knowledge.

Don't Dive into Red Ink

Negative cash flow is a way of life in some areas, especially on the West Coast, where some listings start at $300,000. It's fashionable. Ritzy people buy big fancy

---

* Equity, in case you're new to real estate, means the value of the property minus anything owing on it—in other words, what the owner would have left after selling it and paying off all loans against it with part of the purchase money.

properties they can't pay for—they can't even meet the mortgage payments—so they borrow all over town and pawn their jewels and stall their creditors. They hope to get somewhere down the road by selling at a big enough profit to pay off all those debts, and maybe come out ahead, but usually they end up selling in a hurry because they have to. Sometimes you can buy from one of them if they can afford to be flexible about terms (and if they're not asking an inflated price). How long are you willing to take a loss from a negative cash flow? I'm not willing to take it very long. You shouldn't be either. You don't need to. You can set up your offers so the revenues service the debts.

To do this, your debt payment may have to be smaller (or slower) than standard. Never mind. Forget about standard interest rates when you're buying property. Don't assume that a low interest rate won't be accepted. *Start out with a low offer and give the seller a chance to say yes.*

This shocks the average real-estate agent. Again, never mind. Brokers weren't trained in financing, and the guy who trained them wasn't trained. I'm not running them down, God bless them—they work hard to do the best they know how. But all that many of them know about financing is to call three S & Ls and ask what the rate is. You yourself need to know better ways to work with the seller, or you lose out.

Sellers May Surprise You

I've lost count of the real-estate people who have told me, "Gee, if I'd known the guy would have sold like that, I would have bought it myself." The difference between them and me is that I wrote an offer and they didn't. There are only two answers to an offer, and one of them is great. Have you ever read in the paper that anyone was shot for writing an offer on real estate? I haven't. I've only heard yes or no. The only path to the yeses is through the no's. Don't take the no's personally.

Always take a written offer with you on your first visit to a seller, even though you may rewrite the terms in the course of negotiation. There's a danger in finding a property (especially a good buy) and backing off to think about it. Someone may step in and buy it out from under you.

"Hey, wait!" I hear you saying. "Don't I need time to make sure how much the property is worth? What if he accepts my offer and takes my deposit, and then I find it's a bad deal?"

Defensive Writing

You can still back out without losing your deposit. There's a difference between tying up a property and contracting to buy it. What's the difference? The escape clauses you write into your offer.

You can protect yourself with several of these. Here are a few. (They are not the only ones.)

" . . . subject to inspection and approval by buyer."

" . . . contingent on buyer's approval of an appraisal."

" . . . if approved by buyer's attorney."

" . . . subject to buyer's inspection and approval of books and records." (This is important when you buy apartments or commercial property.)

In fairness to a seller, it is customary to set a time limit to clear these contingencies—usually seven to ten days. You should be able to make a final decision in that time.

Writing an offer doesn't take a lot of work at a typewriter. You can go to an office-supply store and pick up the printed forms that are legal for your state, on which you can just fill in a few blanks to write your offer. Or, if you make an offer through a Realtor, the Board of Realtors will possibly supply its own form.

However, these forms have one thing in common: They all provide plenty of protection for the seller. You need protection too. To get it, you'll need to type in some extra lines on the form (have your attorney run through them, of course).

In addition to the above escape clauses, here are other additions to a standard contract that can benefit you:

Extra Sentences That Help

A. Liability limiter clause, sometimes called an exculpatory clause.

Exculpatory? That's lawyer talk. The word means "freeing from blame." In real estate, an exculpatory clause limits your personal liability. Suppose you can't meet the mortgage payments and you get foreclosed upon. Then, suppose at the foreclosure sale the property sells for less than you owe on it? In some states, the mortgage holder may come after you and get a deficiency judgment, which means that a court orders you to pay the rest out of your assets. You can protect those assets by putting this clause in the mortgage.

The clause might read: "The total liability of this mortgage shall be the building itself, and shall not extend beyond it." It's a simple clause but it gives you, the buyer, a lot of protection. You can insert it after a description of the mortgage.

If the lender objects to the clause, your answer might be, "Do you mean this property is not worth what I'm paying?"

B. Subordination clause.

This is an innocent-looking sentence that could mean a lot of money to you. Let's say when you bought a property you assumed a small first mortgage, and the seller let you create a larger second at low interest to be amortized * over, say, twenty years. Eight or nine years go by. Now the property is worth twice as much (rents are much higher too). Money gets loose, so interest rates drop, and you decide to pull your equity out by refinancing the property. Trouble is, the new lender demands a first mortgage position or else a much higher interest rate. To get the lower rate you'd have to pay off both existing mortgages (otherwise your second would become the first) which would leave you less cash in your pocket after the refinance.

A subordination clause lets you cash out the first mortgage and leave your second in its secondary ("subordinate") position. This will satisfy the new lender. The clause might read:

"The seller's loan shall be subordinate to the existing first mortgage and any renewal, extension or replacement thereof."

Beware of Balloons

C. Extension Clause.

This is a parachute to help you avoid a crash if you're signing a balloon mortgage (a mortgage not amortized, but all due and payable after a certain number of years). When your balloon comes due, you may find yourself in the middle of a tight money market, meaning you'll be forced to pay horrible interest if you try to refinance. This was what burst a lot of balloon borrowers in the late 1970s.

The extension clause gives you time to wait for inter-

---

* "Amortized" is yet another word used constantly in real estate. An amortized loan means that the loan is gradually paid off in equal monthly installments. In amortizing a loan, the bank or other lender figures out the interest for the entire time until the loan is to be paid off, adds this interest to the amount of the loan, and divides the total by the number of payments. As your debt on the property is amortized, your equity (share of ownership) increases.

est rates to come down. It might appear in the contract after a description of the balloon mortgage:

"Seller agrees to extend mortgage for a period not to exceed 18 months, if, in the opinion of the buyer, prevailing interest rates are not low enough to provide a feasible refinance."

A balloon of less than five years is dangerous. This gives you a way to work with sellers who want it.

D. Prospective Tenants Clause.

Look what happens if you write this extra little sentence into your offer form: "Buyer reserves the right to show property to prospective tenants before the closing." Now you write the offer, it is accepted, you can run an ad in the paper and start showing the house. You rent the property before the closing, you get first month's rent and a deposit from the tenant. You take the tenant's cash, not yours, and pay the closing costs. The tenant moves in the day after the closing and you have no lost rent. If for any reason there was no closing, you would, of course, refund the tenant's money.

Who Pays Closing Costs?

E. Closing Costs Clause.

If I'm the buyer, I want the seller to pay the closing costs. Write it in the offer. If the seller says he won't pay all the closing costs, suggest paying half, and ask him to drop the interest down one point on the second mortgage. You have something to negotiate if you've put it in the offer.

F. Broker-Blocking Clause.

As I mentioned in Chapter 7, real-estate brokers prefer to be the sole go-betweens. They don't want to give you a chance to talk the seller into terms that mean less money for them. (Their commission comes from the sale price, remember, and they worry about collecting it if the buyer pays nothing down.) So they may try to insist that you present your offer to them and let them take it alone to their client, the seller.

In that case, just write up your offer and hand it to the broker, but include an extra sentence: "Buyer to accompany broker to present offer." Make it a condition of the contract. Then the broker has to let you come along. Otherwise he can't present your offer. And refusing to present an offer can get a broker in legal trouble. He knows that.

G. Assigns.

It's a simple little word that gives you a lot of options. Put it in. After your name as the buyer, add "or assigns."

"Assigns" is a noun when it's used this way. I don't know why lawyers use it instead of "assignees," which means the same thing. It means someone to whom some rights or interests are or may be transferred.

In your offer, it means that someone you select can take your place as buyer. It lets you bring in a partner with any cash needed to close. It lets you resell the property before closing, or do other things to help yourself.

So much for protection clauses. Now we'll get back to the actual buying plan you'll write into the offer. You can write it in such a way as to give the seller his price and still keep you on the sunny side of the ledger. Let's see how.

Writing the Offer

Remember, we're going to make four assumptions, as explained in Chapter 6.

1. The seller is motivated and flexible. (If he isn't motivated, what are you doing there?)

2. He will sell his property for little or no cash down. (What's a flexible seller for?)

3. He will lend you his equity, through a low-interest mortgage on the property. (Flexible seller again.)

4. He has at least 25 percent equity on the property. (Seller's equity must be large enough to make a reduction in his payment meaningful.)

Conventional lenders aren't going to reduce their terms on the existing loan, especially with interest rates high. So the way to reduce or prevent negative cash flow is to reduce your payments on the seller's portion of the equity. (There's another way, too: I'll show it to you near the end of this chapter.)

The interest rate you pay the seller is negotiable, as I keep saying. Through conversation and your questions, determine as much as possible what the seller's needs are. If he's not talkative, try an approach like this: "There are several ways we can make this work and still give you your price. Let me show you two or three and you tell me what is best for you." Take him through some of the plans I'm about to discuss.

But first, about interest rate. How low do you start? If the seller is highly motivated, offer 6 percent. (Banks aren't ashamed to do it.) He may be thinking in terms of 14 percent. You might settle in the middle around 10.

For the purpose of this chapter we'll assume a seller carry-back interest rate of 10 percent. Your proposal will be different, depending on whether you're buying a rental house or some other kind of income property. Let's consider the house first.

Suppose Mr. Seller wants $100,000 for a house on which he's making monthly payments of $550 against an existing loan of $50,000. For this example, say the rent we can get is $750 a month. We want to buy that house and not have any negative cash flow. The seller's equity is $50,000.

Let's see now. We'll have to take over the $550 monthly payments (the loan is assumable), and we'll need around $100 a month for taxes and miscellaneous expenses. That only leaves $100 of the monthly rental income for servicing our debt on the second mortgage to the seller.

First mortgage payment	$550
Miscellaneous expenses	+ 100
Total outgo so far	650
Rental income	750
Minus outgo (above)	− 650
Remainder so far	$100

These figures show that an amortized loan wouldn't do. Even if spread across twenty years, the payments would be more than the $100 we can count on.

Pay Interest Only?

How about interest only, with the whole principal to be paid after, say, ten years? That won't work in this particular example, as I'll show you in a minute, but in other cases it might be the solution. On a $100,000 loan at 10 percent it would reduce the payments from $1,321.51 a month (10 years amortized) down to $1,000 a month—savings of $321.51 per month.

Interest-only financing is tied to a balloon payment (everything due and payable on a fixed date in the future). A lot of people took what I call short fuses: one- or two-year balloons. When the time was up, borrowers lost property because they couldn't qualify for refinancing, and they had no cash to pay off what they owed. If you want to live the fastest year of your life, take a one-year balloon payment.

Whatever you do, avoid short fuses. Due dates on balloons are negotiable. You want long-term balloons, not short-term. Eight, nine, or ten years, anyway. By then your property should have doubled or more in value, and you'll have no problem paying off. For safety reasons, make the minimum five years. The value will climb enough in five years to let you refinance, pay off the seller's equity and walk away with cash in your pocket.

Coming back to the example we started with, 10 percent interest only for ten years would be $5,000 per year on the seller's equity of $50,000. Divided by twelve months, the monthly interest would be $416.67. But we only have $100. So we need another solution this time.

Less Than Interest Only?

One solution would be split-interest funding. Pay $100 a month interest to the seller and defer the rest of the interest until the loan falls due. In other words, pay $100 and defer $316.67 every month.

If you want a long due date, eight or ten years out, this won't be very attractive to the seller. A better solution would be a graduated payment which you could cover from increases in rent over the years so your revenues would still top your expenses. The offer might be written something like this:

Buyer to assume first mortgage. Seller to carry back a second of $50,000 at 10 percent interest payable as follows:

$100 per month for first year

$200 per month for second year

$300 per month for third year

$400 per month for fourth year

$416.67 per month for the following six years

All principal and unpaid interest to be due and payable in ten years.

Or, let's take another example. $100,000 loan at 12 percent. Instead of offering interest only ($1,000 per month), suppose you offer $800 a month with a five-year balloon. This means you'll owe more money after five years than you do at the start.

How much? $200 paid per month × 5 years (60 months) = $12,000.

In five years a $100,000 property should be worth at least $150,000. That's an average gain in value of only 10 percent a year. So you will have gained $50,000. Subtract the $12,000 extra interest you owe, and your profit is still $38,000. Get a new and bigger loan on the property and cash out your friend the seller. If this is your home or a second home, don't forget to write the $12,000 off your income tax (the '86 tax-law changes let us keep these two interest deductions).

But suppose for some reason the appreciation isn't that much. Suppose refinancing wouldn't produce enough cash to cover the amount you owe.

Okay. Sell the house. Let the new buyer refinance on his own and let his down payment to you make up the additional amount you need ($12,000 in this example). Just give yourself plenty of time to find a buyer. About eighteen months before the balloon comes due, take a look at the property's current value and decide what you're going to do.

Ask for a Moratorium

Moratorium? That's a mouth-filler you may not have come across. It means a "legal authorization to a debtor to suspend payments for a given period."

In your case, after acquiring a property for little or nothing down, it means you would pay nothing more— no interest, no principal—for five years, or whatever period the seller agrees to.

You need a seller with no immediate cash needs but a strong desire to rid himself of the property. You can both profit. Here's how the number might work:

Assume his price is $100,000, and he's making $550 payments on his mortgage. If his equity is $40,000 and you pay him 12 percent interest, just the interest alone would be $400 a month, so you'd need to come up with $950 every month ($550 + $400).

If the house would rent for only $600 to $650 a month, you have a terrific negative cash flow. So you ask the seller for a five-year moratorium on payment to him. This means that in five years $64,000 will be due him ($40,000 principal plus your five years of postponed $400 monthly interest payments, which would add up to $24,000). Let's see what happens if the house appreciates an average of 12 percent per year:

	Now	5 Years From Now:	
House worth	$100,000	$160,000	
You owe	$100,000	$124,000	(his equity plus interest buildup)
Your profit		$ 36,000	

Don't forget that during the five-year period you can take $14,545 in tax write-offs ($80,000 house value without land divided by 27.5 years multiplied by 5 years—assuming you qualify under the new law). Since you have a moratorium on the seller's payments, you will have instant positive cash flow of $50–$100 per month (amount left from rent after you pay the first mortgage). You would, of course, raise the rents perhaps $50 to $75 per year. If you started with $100 per month positive cash flow and raised your rents just $50 per year, you would have a positive cash flow of $12,000 over the five-year period. If you could get four or five of those going, that's a lot of positive cash flow.

Note that as the house appreciates and the seller's equity therefore becomes less of the total value, the risk of this method gets less and has more attraction to you, the buyer.

When the house is worth $160,000, an 80 percent new loan on it would bring you $128,000. You would pay off the old loan and put cash in your pocket.

Don't forget to ask for moratoriums, because some people say yes. Their biggest desire is to get rid of tenant problems, upkeep problems and mortgage payments. I get turned down a lot, but I get yeses, too—and the yeses can make you wealthy.

Try a Combination

This is not a sandwich. It lets you buy the property by solving a problem for the seller.

Suppose the seller is flexible but won't go for a moratorium. Combine the interest-only and split-interest techniques. In the example of the $100,000 loan, we might offer less today when rents are lower and more later when we've raised the rents. For example, our offer might read $750 per month for two years (less than interest only), then $1,000 per month for the next two years (interest only), and $1,200 per month after that (principal plus interest), all due and payable in, say, ten years.

Offer a Tenant a Deal

I've been showing you ways of lowering your monthly payments. Now let's come down to the other side and look at a way of getting a tenant to pay more rent than the going rate.

Why should he do this? Because you offer him part ownership and a share in the profits down the road. Real-estate people call this equity sharing. It's another way to make negative cash flow disappear, while giving yourself a superior tenant.

Remember this: The more you share, the more you make. Let's take an example. Assume we find an excellent investment—a rental house in a good middle-class neighborhood. We can buy it with none of our own cash. The only drawback is, we can only get $500 per month rent while we have to pay $700 per month on the mortgage.

Run an ad like this in the newspaper under homes for rent:

MAKE A HUGE PROFIT AS A RENTER
CALL HOLLIS AT 485-4865

When the phone rings, offer your prospective tenant a half-interest in the house. Set up an escrow, and put in a deed to him for 50 percent ownership based on a contract (drawn by *your* attorney) containing the following:

1. Tenant must agree to live in the house for five years.

2. Tenant agrees to pay $700 per month (not $500, the market rate). No payment can be made more than five days late.

3. Tenant must maintain property in good condition during the period of the contract.

After the five-year period the tenant will have two options:

1. He lets you sell the house and he splits the profits with you.

2. He refinances to generate cash, then gives you half of the increase in the value of the property. The value should be based on MIA appraisal. You select the appraiser. Put it in the contract.

The benefits to you:

1. No negative cash flow.

2. No management problems. You have an owner living in the house.

3. No rent-collection problem. Tenant must pay on time or lose his equity in the house.

4. There is no limit to the number of partners you can acquire, each in a different home.

Benefits to the tenant:

1. Half a home is better than none.

2. Ultimately he can use his profits to buy all of this home or another. It's much better than trying to save up for a big down payment.

3. No down payment is needed. (Great for young couples just starting.)

During the five-year period, *you* own the home and get all the tax benefits of ownership (depreciation and property tax write-offs). Another way would be to give the tenant half the house immediately and give him half the tax benefits.

Of course there's some risk. You're signing a contract. If the tenant doesn't live up to the contract, or he says you're not living up to it, you could get into a lawsuit.

So what? If you're looking for headache-free investments, stay away from real estate. If you even find a way to make half a million dollars with absolutely no headaches, call me collect. I'd love to go into business with you. Meanwhile, I'd rather have wealth with a few problems than no wealth. Think about it!

Making Offers on Income Property

Now let's move along to ways of staying in the black when buying income property bigger than a single-family house. By that I mean anything from a duplex or small apartment building all the way up to skyscrapers and major shopping centers.

As far as avoiding negative cash flow is concerned, your offer will be structured basically the same as for a house. However, you have to be more careful about determining your break-even point. You know what your debt service will cost, but you're not sure about other expenses, so you can't tell how much of the rental income will be left over. You need to arrive at a safe estimate.

A real-estate broker will hand you an income-expense sheet which supposedly lists all of the operating costs. Be very wary. Sellers are known for sins of omission (expenses left out). This may not be intentional, but how is a broker to know exactly what a property's expenses are? They're not his expenses, they're the seller's expenses.

Let me give you a guideline that will help you write offers on income property. For an apartment building, your cost of operation will be roughly 25 percent of its gross income *plus* its property taxes.

If the property taxes ran 20 percent of the gross, your cost of running then would be 45 percent of the gross (25 percent plus 20 percent). In this country, actual property taxes run from around 10 percent of the gross income to over 30 percent. That's why you have to separate the taxes.

Exceptions to the Guideline

The 25 percent number is based on assumptions about utility costs and damage expenses. Here's what I mean.

1. We're assuming that the tenants pay the utility bills except for common areas like a patio or lobby and halls. If the utility bills paid by the property are more than 2 or 3 percent of the gross, add the excess to your 25 percent figure.

Example: Utilities were 8 percent of the gross income. Subtract 3 percent from the 8 percent and get 5 percent excess. Add this to your 25 percent base and get 30 percent. So your cost of running the building would be 30 percent of the gross plus property taxes.

2. We're assuming that few children live in the apartments. If a building has mostly two-bedroom and three-bedroom units, you'll have more kids and more damage. So add 2 or 3 percent to the figure. Your cost to operate would be 28 percent of the gross income plus the property taxes.

Sample Operating Project

Here's how the numbers might work out in an actual example.

Imagine a 10-unit apartment building. Half of the units are two-bedroom, renting at $400 a month. Half are one-bedroom units at $300.

The price tag on this property is $250,000 with nothing down. The seller's equity is $100,000. So he still owes $150,000 on it, and his mortgage payments are $18,000 per year.

The gross is $42,000 a year—$2,000 a month from the $400 apartments and $1,500 a month from the $300 units, which adds up to $3,500 a month ($3,500 × 12 = $42,000).

The property taxes are $6,300 a year, we'll say, and utilities are $1,000 a year.

Given these figures, how much can you pay the seller per month and still break even on the cash flow? Remember, the key items are utilities and property taxes!

Property taxes figure out to 15 percent of the gross income ($6,300 divided by $42,000 = .15, or 15 percent).

We figured that the utilities are $1,000, which is 2.38 percent of the gross ($1,000 divided by $42,000). Since the utilities are less than 3 percent of the gross, we don't have to add any percentage to our 25 percent base.

Our formula gives us 40 percent of the gross income as the cost of running the building (the 25 percent base plus 15 percent for taxes). This leaves 60 percent of our rental income to cover debt service.

We said the gross income is $42,000. When we take 60 percent of that amount we get $25,200 a year we can afford for debt service.

But the lending institutions get $18,000 of this, leaving only $7,200 ($600 per month) for our payments on the second mortgage. Is this enough to amortize the second? No.

Would interest-only payments keep the cash flow coming our way? Since the seller's equity is $100,000, if we assume a 10 percent interest rate we'll owe him $10,000 a year, or $833.33 per month in cash. The $600 per month we've allowed still leaves us a little short.

Then we'll have to write a split-interest funding offer.

Split Interest Keeps You Out of the Red

Suppose you offer to pay the seller $500 per month. That's 6 percent interest ($500 per month = $6,000 per year). Remember we're still assuming no down payment, a first mortgage of $150,000, which you must assume, and a second mortgage of $100,000 at 10 percent. Ask him to defer the other 4 percent. This deferred interest, plus the principal, are to fall due in ten years (take nine, five, six, seven or eight years due date—it will still work).

This will net you $100 a month after all costs, providing your formula of 25 percent of gross plus property tax holds up, as it should, barring a disaster. So you'll have a $100 cushion for a few rental delinquencies or vacant apartments.

Maybe the seller won't go for deferring 4 percent interest. Maybe he'll only defer 3 percent. Even so, your 7 percent payments will be just $583.33 per month. You have a little cash left each month.

And remember, you're only one rent raise away from a really comfortable cash flow. And when income-tax time rolls around, you can take the building's depreciation deduction (assuming you qualify under the '86 guidelines of management and maximum deduction). That will cause the IRS to refund part of your tax dollars. This, plus the other tax benefits, can be like the duck dropping down on "You Bet Your Life." The fairy godmother appearing in a burst of sparkles. Tinker Bell. The jackpot in Reno.

Don't Forget the Specialists

The sample offers in this chapter are guidelines, not blueprints. They do *not* take the place of attorneys and CPAs. A property may have hidden flaws, or a seller may be tricky, and you need protection in the contract. Then, too, I haven't mentioned many clauses that will benefit you if you can get them. And the CPA is the one who should figure your taxes. Please use these people when you're involved with contracts and/or taxation.

12

TRAPPED BY A BALLOON? STRATEGIES FOR ESCAPE

WE LOOKED AT BALLOON MORTGAGES IN CHAPTER 11. Now let's think more about them. First a quick review.

When conventional lenders such as banks and S & Ls take a second mortgage, they sometimes set the interest rate as low as if it were amortized over 30 years, but the bulk of the principal (called the balloon payment) comes due in only three to five years. That's one kind of balloon mortgage.

Other kinds are those you yourself can negotiate with flexible sellers: interest only, split interest (less than interest only), zero interest. In Chapter 11, I suggested using these to spread your capital so you could buy a lot of properties instead of just a few.

I even showed you how to structure your purchases so you wouldn't use much (if any) of your own capital, by making sure the properties' cash flow would cover your debt service and other monthly costs. Of course, that still leaves the problem of paying the principal when the due date rolls around. Have you noticed that the older you get, the faster the years slip by? If you want to live the fastest year of your life, take a balloon mortgage due in one year.

I warned you: Never, ever gamble on a short fuse—a one- or two-year balloon. This doesn't allow enough time for property to appreciate and put you within reach of cash to pay the balloon by refinancing. A big short-term debt means you'll probably lose the property. Or if you do find a wad of cash and pay off, it's almost like an all-cash buy. You won't get wealthy that way.

You *can* build financial independence on balloon mortgages of eight or ten years. They're practically risk-less. Remember my rule of thumb: The shortest safe balloon is five years. In that time the property should become worth much more than you owe. Then you can pocket a profit either by refinancing or reselling. (Reselling cuts off your probably bigger profit down the road, so I don't urge you to do it unless you need cash.)

Still, I can't promise that five years will bring you a profit ten times out of ten. There are exceptions to most rules, including my rule about five-year balloons.

Downdrafts Can Hurt You

Probably you've heard tales that freeze your heart about people who bought a house on a five-year mortgage only to lose the house (and all the interest they'd paid) at the end of the five years. Most buyers who lost had three-year mortgages, but there were some fives that turned sour in the late 1970s when mortgage rates went out of sight. Young families who wanted to buy a home thought the only way they could afford it was via balloon.

This meant they were betting they could borrow more at lower rates from a bank (or at worst from a finance company), when the balloon fell due. They couldn't. Mortgage rates dropped, but not far enough. Their houses weren't worth much more before as collateral, partly because of the recession, and partly because a speculative house-buying binge (in boom areas like parts of California and Texas) had bid prices way up beyond value. The prices had to sink back for a while.

Could something like that happen to you? Will a five-year mortgage really keep you safe?

Usually, but not always. You might have bought in a good neighborhood only to see the zoning subsequently changed and a half-block excavated for a high-rise. Or there has been a traffic-pattern shift, and your street is now full of horns and headlights. Or some other bad things have happened. In extreme cases real estate does lose value instead of appreciating. Rents do go down here and there.

And now there's a question about inflation, which we count on to keep values climbing. Prices have been rising for centuries. Through most of the 1970s the inflation rate was double digit. In 1983 inflation slowed down. In 1984 prices rose at only 5 to 6 percent. However, most economists don't see that low rate lasting.

We needn't ignore bad possibilities. It's always best to know what we'll do if the dam breaks or the markets crash. Let's sketch the worst case scenarios, and see how you can arrange happy endings.

No Inflation? You Win Anyway!

Suppose the gloom-and-doomers are right. Say you go out in the next few years and buy (without using your cash) a million dollars' worth of income property. The day after your last closing, inflation stops. (It really did stop for a few years back in the 1930s, during the worst of the Great Depression. We even had a whiff of deflation.) We'll assume land prices stay where they are, or even drop. Same for building materials, house prices and apartment rents.

Are you ruined? Far from it. You merely hold on to your million dollars' worth of property. A group of very nice people (your tenants) sit in your property and buy the property for you while you enjoy the tax shelters and cash flow. After, say, twenty-five years, you are worth one million dollars, the properties are paid off and you are wealthy because these are valuable dollars. (Remember, inflation stopped!)

Balloon Due? What to Do

But we haven't yet looked at the problem of what to do if your balloon due date is approaching, with no cash in sight to pay off. You want to hold the property but you're in danger of being foreclosed.

Naturally you won't wait until you're delinquent before you head into your planned escape route. In fact, you'll start at least a year ahead, to give yourself time to maneuver.

This will be easier if you have put a protective clause in the original contract of sale, as I suggested in Chapter 11: "Seller agrees to extend mortgage for a period not to exceed 18 months, if, in the opinion of the buyer, prevailing interest rates are not low enough to provide a feasible refinance."

Even if you didn't get this clause into the contract, trying for an extension is one of your options. It's probably the best choice in a tight money market when refinancing would be too expensive.

Go see the seller long before he starts wondering whether you're in trouble. Don't ask him for help—offer him something he'll like.

You might begin by pointing out that when he collects your balloon payment he'll owe the IRS a hefty tax. Would he like to stretch that taxable event out for several years? If he's interested, show him how to do this by postponing the due date of your balloon. Try for a postponement of two or three years.

He may even prefer to think in terms of an amortized loan where his tax is spread over *many* years! If so, work out a whole new loan agreement with him. Get your CPA to help figure the payment schedule.

On the other hand, the seller may scowl at your first mention of delaying the balloon. This means you'll have to sweeten the pot. Offer him a higher interest rate in return for an extension. If he's a tough bargainer he may demand not only higher payments, but a fee for renewal.

The fee could take the form of points (one point equals 1 percent of the loan amount).

You're probably not in a strong bargaining position if money is tight. You may have to agree to most of what he wants. (If you can't afford it, see Chapter 8 on ways to buy if you're cash poor; Chapter 9 on sources of down payments and dealing with lenders; Chapter 10 on establishing good credit quickly. Some of the tips in these chapters will help you raise more capital when you need it.)

Paying points and higher interest may be about as much fun as having a root canal. But look at what you're trying to accomplish. You are buying time. Time will move you into a position where you can refinance for an amortized loan and blow away your balloon problem.

Three More Inducements You Can Offer

But before you agree to the seller's demands—maybe before he even makes them—think about three other deals you may be able to offer him. Here they are.

1. Help him buy more property.

Many months before the loan is due, ask your mortgage holder if he would like to buy a piece of real estate with your note. (If he needs tax shelter he may agree.) Explain that motivated sellers will often take paper (mortgages) for a down payment. Many of them will accept the paper at full face value (no discount). If he's interested, locate the purchase for him. Better yet, locate it first, so you can tell him about it when you suggest the idea. In return, you want him to extend the terms of the mortgage for a few years. In other words:

(a) You get an extended note.

(b) The motivated seller of the other property gets that note.

(c) Your note holder gets a piece of property for needed tax shelter.

(d) All three parties are happy. It's all win/win!

2. A subordination agreement is a contract between debtor and creditor in which a creditor agrees that the claims of a certain other creditor will become "senior" —that is, they must be paid in full before any payment can be made to the subordinate creditor. The agreement becomes important in case of foreclosure. Whoever holds the senior mortgage will collect the proceeds of the foreclosure sale, and the holder of the subordinate mortgage will get what's left over after the senior claim is paid.

You can ask your seller to subordinate (step down to the junior position) to a new first mortgage on the property. This will allow you to get a much higher new loan from a bank or S & L, since it will be recorded as holding top priority, and you won't have to pay off the second mortgage. It also gives you a nice lump of cash. You use part of this to pay off part of the balloon. That's inducement to the seller. How much of your cash does he get? It's negotiable! Start with a low offer and negotiate from there. You give the seller part of his note in cash and a higher interest rate on the remainder he will still carry (an inducement to accept your offer).

3. Raise the amount of the second.

Instead of reducing your mortgage, you add to it. Let's say the balloon mortgage was $45,000. You might offer to raise the mortgage to $50,000 and tack on the same interest payment for several years more. Again, you are paying money to buy time. That isn't the most favorable solution for you, but it sure beats foreclosure as an option.

Sometimes You Can Refinance

Refinancing during a tight money market with 17 or 18 percent interest rates isn't an attractive solution. Conventional lenders won't even talk about it in such times unless your collateral is like emeralds or your credit is as good as a Rockefeller's. But times change, and those collar-size interest rates can shrink. Maybe the money market is on its best behavior when your balloon date looms ahead. Then you may get a better deal from a bank or S & L than from your mortgage holder. It's worth trying.

If the balloon payment is a second mortgage, ask about refinancing the property, getting a big enough mortgage to cash out the existing first and second mortgages and perhaps to put some money in your wallet. How big a loan you get depends on what the property's existing rents at the time will carry—or, if it's your home, what payments your bank account can stand.

If the terms of the first mortgage are attractive, you might keep it (again we're supposing the balloon mortgage is a second) and just get a new second. If we're talking about rental property, your rental income is surely higher now than when you signed the purchase contract. Therefore you may be able to afford slightly higher payments. Or if the property is your own home, maybe your salary has gone up.

Look at getting an amortized second over, say, seven to ten years. Maybe your income will pay it off without the need to hook yourself into any balloon this time.

Find a Private Lender

Believe it or not, there are plenty of rich people looking for ways to put their surplus wealth to work. To cater to them, all major newspapers run a Sunday column of classified ads headed "Money Wanted." People with money to lend read the column. Know this: Smart borrowers put ads there.

Take an ad and find the funds to pay off your balloon by creating a new mortgage. A friend of mine ran a three-dollar ad in a local newspaper just a few years ago and got a $100,000 mortgage, due in ten years. He paid 10 percent interest only. Don't be shy—advertise!

If all else fails, and you are facing foreclosure on your own home, deed 5 percent of it to anyone in the Armed Forces (nephew, cousin, maybe just a friend). Then apply for relief from foreclosure under the Soldiers and Sailors Civil Relief Act. The mere mention of the act puts fear into lenders. For openers, this act won't let the lender charge more than 6 percent interest. If you've been paying 12 to 15 percent, this starts to look attractive!

You Can Learn to Love Balloons!

Remember, there are two main reasons to commit yourself to a balloon mortgage:

1. To reduce your monthly payments in the early years of the loan, letting you buy property with payments you can afford.

2. To encourage the lender to make the loan by shortening the time his money is tied up. Even some S & Ls now don't like to tie up capital for thirty years.

Once you realize there are ways to handle balloon payments when they come due, you start to lose your fear of this kind of short-term debt. And you begin to see it as an investment vehicle you can use.

I've shown you several ways of restructuring this debt if you can't pay it when due. But they aren't the only ways. Don't be limited by what you have read or heard. Get in the habit of trying to think up new and different solutions to your problems. The more you practice, the more inventive you'll get!

13

UNDERSTANDING RATE OF RETURN

"I CAN'T GET ANY CASH FLOW SO I'M NOT MAKING ANY-thing on my money. How can you say I'm building wealth?" After a lecture, many people come up to me and ask this question or some variation of it. They still feel cash poor. Yet, if they only knew, their wealth is increasing steadily.

The trouble is, they don't understand rate of return. They confuse cash flow with "making something on their money." How about you? Do you understand rate of return?

Rate of return means total payback, total increase in wealth. Some of this increase may be temporarily invisible because the cash isn't in your hands yet. But it does just as much for you financially in the course of a year. The rental money your properties bring in (the cash flow) is only one part of your rate of return.

The Formula for Rate of Return

Let's analyze rate of return, so you'll understand the staggering long-term profits you can legally make as a real-estate investor.

To put it in a mathematical formula, Rate of Return equals Money Made divided by Money Invested.

"Money Invested" is easy. That's the down payment plus closing costs. (Some closing costs can be greatly reduced, once you know how.)

"Money Made" is more complex. It is made up of four factors:

1. Cash flow. That is, your net cash from the rent income after paying expenses and debt service.

2. Tax savings. Money you keep instead of paying out in taxes, because of the depreciation write-off.

3. Equity buildup. Remember, your equity is the percentage of the property's cost that you've paid. With each installment on the mortgage you build up your equity by paying down part of the principal.

4. Appreciation. How much the property's value has risen since you bought it. Of course you can only estimate this unless you get an up-to-date appraisal, or put the property on the market, or refinance it. Realtors can give you a pretty close estimate any time.

So! Rate of Return is

$$\frac{\text{Appreciation } + \text{ Equity Buildup } + \text{ Tax Savings } + \text{ Cash Flow}}{\text{Money Invested}}$$

How to Calculate Your Rate

Let's take an actual example and work out the various parts of the top line in the formula.

We'll use round numbers to make it easier. Imagine you own a $100,000 rental property. The land, which isn't depreciable, is worth $20,000. The property on it is worth $80,000. You bought it with a $20,000 down payment.

You're renting it for $1,600 a month. But you have to pay $800 a month on the mortgage or mortgages. Furthermore, the cost of upkeep and other operating expenses average another $800 a month, we'll say. In that case your cash flow is zero. That's why you think you're not earning anything on your investment.

But what about appreciation? Let's estimate 10 percent per year. This could be a low figure in the mid-to-
late 1980s, when the housing shortage is likely to become
hellacious. In 1983 housing prices slumped in some areas
(as they do in most recessions). This was an abnormally
slow year for real estate, with a few cities like Houston
feeling the effects of a temporary surplus in housing.
Even so, the nationwide appreciation rate for that year
was around 5 percent. The National Association of
Homebuilders says the average new house in the U.S.
currently costs $75,300. The average a year ago was
$70,800. So new houses have appreciated 6.4 percent on
the average. And the National Association of Realtors
says the average resale price of an existing home right
now is $70,400. A year ago it was $67,700, which equals
about a 4 percent rise. These are very conservative
estimates. And remember that, historically, housing
prices have always shown an extra big rise after a year
or two of subnormal gains. For the past quarter-century
the uptrend has averaged well above 10 percent a
year.

Whatever the appreciation in this particular imagi-
nary case, it isn't money in your pocket until you sell or
refinance. But it's still an addition to your net worth. So
you need to take it into account when figuring how your
investment is doing. And in this example we'll calculate
it at $10,000.

Equity Buildup

In the early years of a loan, most of your payment
goes for interest, and there's less reduction of principal
than in the later years. The bank or S & L gives you a
monthly statement showing exactly how much you've
paid down the principal so far. If you want to know how
much more equity you'll own a year from now, you can
look at amortization tables available in almost any finan-

cial or real-estate office. For our purpose, let's say you've whittled down the principal (built up your equity) by 2½ percent this year. All right, 2½ percent of the $80,000 value of the loan equals $2,000. That's the amount we factor into our equation.

Don't Forget the Tax Saving

The 1986 tax law changes allow 27.5-year straight-line depreciation on residential property. In other words, you assume that the building loses 1/27.5 of its total value each year.

We know, and the IRS knows, that the building probably becomes more valuable, rather than less, as time passes. But Congress still wants to encourage real-estate investment by the small investor, so it left depreciation on the books up to a maximum of $25,000 for those who are actually involved with their properties. Other tax deductions against income of the property, such as operating expenses and property taxes, are just a compensation for hard cash you've had to pay out. But you don't need any expenditure or loss to get the depreciation write-off.

As we did before, to figure this write-off, divide the property's $80,000 value by 27.5. This means your depreciation deduction is $2,909.

If we assume you're in the 28 percent bracket (maximum after 1987), your actual tax saving is $814. Note that any tax savings is really an addition to your cash flow since taxes saved can be spent immediately.

You needn't wait until April 15 to add this saving to your spendable cash. If you're employed, you can refigure your tax and have your employer reduce the amount withheld from your salary checks. If you're self-employed or retired and filing quarterly estimates (with payments) just change your estimate and pay less each quarter.

Anyhow, we now have all the factors in the equation:

Your Rate of Return = $10,000 Appreciation + $2,000 Equity Buildup + $814 Tax Saving + 0 Cash Flow, all divided by $20,000 Money Invested. Reducing this to only the numbers, we have:

$$R \text{ of } R = \frac{\$10,000 + \$2,000 + \$814 + 0}{\$20,000}$$

Add up the numbers and we get $R \text{ of } R = \dfrac{\$12,814}{\$20,000}$ which equals 64 percent as the rate of return. Do any other investments pay you 64 percent a year?

Look What Leverage Does

Now observe the miracle of leverage. If you can make a smaller down payment without raising the monthly payment, what happens to the rate of return on your invested capital?

For $10,000 down, $R \text{ of } R = \dfrac{12,814}{10,000} = 128$ percent

For $5,000 down, $R \text{ of } R = \dfrac{12,814}{5,000} = 256$ percent

For $1,000 down, $R \text{ of } R = \dfrac{12,814}{1,000} = 1,281$ percent

I've taken you through this rate of return formula because it highlights three important benefits to your creation of wealth:

1. The great big zero for cash flow, which we've used in the example, shouldn't stay at zero in the second year. Remember, you're going to raise your rents about once a year. Even under adverse conditions like rent control you're allowed a percentage increase every year (see section on rent control).

2. Equity buildup, like cash flow, increases with time.

This, too, increases your rate of return as the years go by.

3. The smaller your down payment, the bigger the return on your invested dollar. You get wealthier faster, in other words.

14

A FAIRLY SIMPLE
WAY TO RETIRE EARLY
AND PUT KIDS
THROUGH COLLEGE

USING THE METHOD I'M ABOUT TO EXPLAIN, YOU CAN generate an income of more than $50,000 per year after just three or four years. More income? Use this method on more and more properties. Or just use it for more years.

The method involves combining two techniques: (1) a lease-option purchase; (2) an interest-only down-payment sale. The first of these may be entirely new to you, so let's consider it in detail. You really ought to understand it and use it often, because it gives you so many money-making advantages in buying and selling single-family rental homes.

What a Lease-Option Is

A lease, of course, is a legally binding agreement in writing. An owner agrees to let a renter use or occupy property while paying a fixed monthly rent for it during a stated period of time. During this time the owner can't raise the rent. And the renter must keep on paying.

An option is the purchased privilege of either buying or selling something at a specified price within a specified time. In this case, the prospective buyer (optionee) has the option. The owner (optionor) simply promises to hold the offer open for the length of time agreed. He gives this promise in return for a cash consideration, which can be as little as one dollar. He can't sell to anyone else during the option period. If the optionee does buy the property, the amount he paid for the option usually becomes the deposit on the purchase price. If he doesn't buy, he loses the deposit.

Put the lease and the option together, and you have a lease (or agreement to rent) combined with a privilege of buying during a future period.

You agree to lease and the seller agrees to let you buy. You have to honor the lease. But you don't have to buy. That's at your option.

What's Good About It

A lease-option (often called a "lease with option to buy") is a great way to control property without putting up much money, and to lock in some profit from its appreciation—while still keeping the old financing, and thereby keeping your cash flow positive, rather than negative (which would mean more cash going out than coming in).

And how about young renters? Look what a lease-option can do for them.

They can move into a $75,000 house and have a monthly payment of only $450 or so. It's more affordable than the monthly payment on a conventional purchase, which might be in the $700–$800 range. And they've tied up the property for several years, during which their income is likely to increase. And they can afford a higher payment. As for the owner, he's probably happy with such an arrangement. He gets market or above-market rent from good tenants who have maximum incentive to keep the property in good condition because they plan to purchase it. People don't tear up property they're going to own. Nor do they walk away from a large rent credit toward the purchase price—so the seller is practically assured of the sale.

For investors who want to work with expensive homes worth $300,000 and up, the lease-option is a way to bring their monthly payment on these homes down to the $1,500-per-month level, instead of the usual $3,000-up range on a conventional purchase. In other words, it enables them to buy property they might not be able to finance by any other method. It also brings the payment down to a level where market rent can cover it.

It's surprising how few people know about these advantages. Most investors, and their real estate brokers, never think of using a lease-option.

The buyers and sellers probably never heard of it. The agents don't fully understand it and don't even like to think about it, because they don't receive their full sales commission until (and unless) the option is exercised later on.

A Hedge Against Deflation

Maybe you're skeptical, or at least concerned, because real-estate prices have gone up a lot in the last years. In some areas they tripled during the 1970s; in some places they doubled within a three-year period. Now you think this seems too good to continue. You wonder what will happen if prices turn down. Can you be stuck with a property that isn't even worth the amount of the mortgage?

Well, I have good news for you. You can make money if a house appreciates. Or you can make money if the house never appreciates. And even if prices actually sink, you still won't be stuck. You win wherever prices go, if you lease with an option to buy.

Here's an example of how this works.

A house is for sale at $75,000. The owners are motivated. They are in a hurry to sell, but have no particular need for cash.

They are making payments on an older 9 percent

FHA loan, made originally for $40,000. FHA loans are fully assumable just by signing your name. If you take it over, it will cost you altogether $400 per month PITI (Principal, Interest, Tax on the property, and Insurance on the property).

You tell the owners, "I'll pay you $450 per month on a lease with an option to buy after four years." To buy for how much? As usual, it's negotiable. If you say $85,000, it may look wonderful to the owners, who were asking only $75,000.

By giving you the lease and an option, the owners accomplish two things. They get the house off their hands (their primary concern) and they receive a $50 monthly cash flow ($450 − $400 FHA payment) during the four-year period of the lease. So the papers are signed.

Now you sublet that house to someone for $475 a month. Then *you* start out with a $25 monthly positive cash flow. At the end of a year you raise the rent $50 per month. Rent raises should get easier in the late 1980s, because the worst of the housing shortage is yet to come.

With the tenants paying $525 a month, your net cash intake rises to $75 a month. At the end of the second year, you raise your rent another $50, so your cash flow becomes $125. A year later you up the rent again by the same amount, so your cash flow is $175 per month ($125 + $50). During the entire four years, your net cash intake totals $4,800.

Now the lease expires and it's "option to buy" time. Did the house appreciate?

It did? Is it worth more than $85,000? If so, great! Let's exercise our option and buy it, and take the extra profit.

But maybe the house turns out to be worth *less* than $85,000 at option time. No problem. We let the option expire. We walk away and keep all the $4,800 we received.

The point is, if the house appreciates, the lease-option lets you make money by exercising your option. If the house doesn't appreciate, you've made money anyhow from the rent payments. Since you have the choice of buying or not buying, you can't lose.

One further fact about inflation and real-estate prices. Most people think a lower rate of inflation (such as in 1983) must hurt the investment performance of real estate. But John McMahan, a San Francisco real-estate consultant, studied the data and found that this belief is wrong. His study, reported in *The Wall Street Journal,* showed that real estate's performance doesn't vary greatly between periods of low and high inflation. The "real return" on real estate (that is, the inflation-adjusted return, or the amount your dollars will buy) rose 11.2 percent during the highly inflationary years of 1969–78, compared with an annual rise of 9.6 percent during 1951–68, a period of low inflation.

So, I can't see any excuse for not investing in real estate. You can structure lease-option transactions to make money regardless of the economy or the future of real-estate prices.

Four Steps to an Ample Income

Now let's get back to the method for generating a retirement income.

Step One: Find a $250,000 house owned by a motivated seller.

It must be old enough so the property has doubled in value. How old is that? Say seven to ten years, depending on the area. You want an older property because you want the payment on the original loan to be low enough for you to afford. Let's say the payment on this house is $1,200 per month—the same payment established when the house sold for $125,000 new.

Step Two: Offer the owner a lease with option to buy, and get him to accept it.

The lease and the option should be for four years. During that time, the lease binds you to pay $1,200 per month, which the owner uses to make the mortgage payment. And at the end of the four years, if you exercise the option, you are to deliver the balance of the $250,000 price to the seller in cash. You say you haven't got a quarter-million and don't expect to have it? Never mind. You'll see how it will come.

The $1,200 monthly lease payment is to apply to the purchase price of the house. So the amount of the final payment due at option time will be reduced by the lease payments. Let's see—you pay $1,200 per month for 48 months, for a total of $57,600. So you'll owe $192,400 at the end of four years.

Step Three: Now comes the second technique I mentioned at the start of this chapter: the interest-only down-payment sale.

As soon as you've leased the house, you put it up for sale on a "contract of sale" (in your state it may be called a "contract for deed" or some other name). You have to sell it that way because you don't yet have title to the property. You'll get title when you exercise your option.

Maybe you're saying, "It sounds risky, trying to buy and sell property that I don't have title to." If you have a contract for sale, and you have a deed conveying title sitting in an escrow office (I'll explain that later in the chapter) you don't have any title problems.

You're going to turn around and sell this house for $255,000 or just $5,000 more than your option lets you buy it for. Run the following ad in the newspaper:

$255,000 house for sale

$5,000 down

$250,000 private loan, interest only, at 10%

You will get calls. Many potential buyers of a quarter-million-dollar home don't have the normal down payment of at least $25,000 but can afford the payment you ask.

Structure this interest-only sale so the balloon payment will fall due in, say, 45 months (three months before your option expires). Here's how it is set up:

The down payment (2 percent) is $5,000.

The monthly payment (10 percent interest on $250,000) is $25,000 per year, or $2,083 per month.

The balloon payment (the $250,000 principal) is due in 3¾ years.

Step Four: Sit back and wait for the 45 months to pass. Your work is over.

No More Work, but Nice Pay

Meanwhile you're being compensated for waiting. You're collecting an interest-only payment of $2,083 per month, from which you turn over $1,200 per month in lease payments to the owner.

In other words, you net $883 per month with no work. In a year, that comes to $10,596 ($883 × 12). Over the 45 months it adds up to a grand total of $39,735.

There's even more profit down the road, because your payments on the lease-option have all been going toward principal. You've built up equity while you waited. The whole $250,000 due to you hasn't been reduced at all, because the payments you collected were interest only. So here's what happens:

Your buyer hands you $250,000 when it comes due at the end of 45 months. From this you give the original seller only $196,000 because you've already paid him $54,000 ($1,200 per month for 45 months). His $250,000 minus your $196,000 to the seller leaves you with $54,000 minus a few closing costs.

Altogether, then, your net profit on the transaction is about $93,735 (the $54,000 plus the $39,735 interest you've received). You made almost $100,000 by knowing how to package real estate.

Note: Does a $250,000 transaction sound scary to you? Then start with a $50,000 or $75,000 or $100,000 house. The price doesn't matter. As you get used to the method, you can take over as many houses as you find flexible owners.

The example I've described is a "perfect" example. In the real world, with everything negotiable, maybe your profit will be cut to only $50,000 because a seller insists on a higher price, or because he won't agree that your entire rent payment will apply to the purchase.

Even so, isn't it a nice way to net $50,000 with little or none of your own money involved?

Acquire and sell just one house a year on such terms, and your income is $50,000 a year. Finding the seller and buyer, and negotiating the terms may take you a total of one month yearly. The other eleven months you can sleep till noon, throw away your clocks, and go sailing or golfing.

How to Persuade Owners

Chances to arrange a lease with option to buy can be found in the newspapers almost daily. Any owner who advertises "little or nothing down" is a possibility.

Look under "Houses for Rent Unfurnished." Call up those advertisers. At least one in ten, maybe more, will agree to your proposal after they get over their surprise at discovering you want to buy instead of rent.

Here's one way to ease into the negotiations: "I'm looking for a home that I can rent now and buy later. How would you feel about that?" If they intend to hold on to their property, they'll tell you immediately. But owners who are primarily investors are usually interested in an easy way to cash in their profits. Some may have tried to sell but found no takers.

Another way to start the negotiation: "If I give you a three-year lease, would you consider giving me an option to buy?" The standard lease is for only one year. Owners who've had trouble with tenant turnover may be glad that you'll commit for three years, even though they lose the chance to raise the rent.

Instead of asking questions like the above, some negotiators prefer to talk rather tough at the beginning. "If I take all the management problems of this property off your hands and give you a three-to-five-year lease, will you lower my rent by a hundred dollars a month and give me an option to buy?" It's a negotiating tactic sometimes called a shuffle. They don't really think the owner will cut the rent. But after they yield on this, the owner may find the rest of their proposal more reasonable by contrast.

In most kinds of business a prospective buyer has to pay something (a "consideration") for an option. But in real estate a lease is often enough consideration. The payment is negotiable. Some optionees pay $5,000. Some pay $50. The reason some pay $50 is because that's what they offer. You can start by offering $1. All a contract requires is a dollar. The more motivated the seller, the less you pay in front for a lease-option.

Beating the Due-on-Sale Clause

Here's one more use of the lease-option. Let's say you have one of the older, lower-interest mortgages on your property. You want to sell. But prospective buyers can't afford the higher interest on current mortgages, and can't assume the old mortgage because it contains a due-on-sale clause which effectively forces your buyer to pay off the old mortgage and take on a new one.

The buyer's way out (and yours) is a lease-option. Let's say the old mortgage has fifteen years to run. You set up a fifteen-year lease with an option to buy. Long-term leases are common in certain situations, such as when a buyer wants to retain the advantages of the old financing.

The title to the property stays in your name. The insurance policy stays, too. How can the lender call the loan? I've never heard of a lender trying to do so, and I'm pretty sure there are no court decisions permitting this. Of course, you'll want to make the paperwork airtight, which means it should be drawn up by a skilled, knowledgeable real estate attorney. Notice I said "real estate attorney." If real estate isn't his specialty, you're in the wrong office. After choosing an attorney, you might help him by suggesting he look up IRS Revenue Ruling 55-540, Section 4.05. This will give him some referral cases and favorable court rulings.

Even though ownership won't pass for many years, the attorney may be able to help you pass along the tax benefits of ownership to the lessor. These benefits hinge on what the parties intended. If the lease finds the lessor into the purchase, the wording can show that this intent is a big factor in arriving at the sale price the lessor is to pay. In other words, if the parties intended to make a sale by using the lease-option devices, this entitles the lessor to the tax benefits. Again, consult your real-estate attorney.

How to Protect a Lease-Option

1. Don't rely on verbal agreements or loosely worded memos. After a few years, memories get amazingly changeable, especially if the house's value has rocketed. The basic agreement between you and the seller should spell out the terms and conditions of the lease—and of the purchase which will follow in a few years.

For example, if the seller is going to carry a mortgage on the house after the purchase, the lease should specify the length of time, interest rate and monthly payment.

2. Always put a "right to sublet" clause in your lease-

purchase contracts. This means that you and the owner must strike out the section in most printed lease-option contracts which calls for prior written consent of the owner before subleasing. Everyone involved must initial this change.

Sometimes a smart owner will demand the right to screen your prospective tenant. (He's afraid you may sublet to an immigrant family who will then invite eighteen needy relatives to move in, too. It has happened.) If this question comes up, make sure the provision to screen contains sections that say any rejection must be based on "reasonable" grounds, and the owner must decide on the tenant's suitability "without unreasonable delay."

Remember, there are no routine lease agreements. You'll hear people say that their lease, mortgage or other printed document is a "standard" form. Any standard form is likely to be lopsided in favor of the person who offers it to you. A good attorney should help you draw up your own lease agreement.

3. Have the seller sign a deed to the property and put it in a neutral depository (an escrow) with a clause saying it is to be delivered to you when you exercise your option.

4. Get the lease-option agreement notarized. Then have it properly recorded with the appropriate local government office. Usually this will be the county recorder or the city clerk. (For a small fee, a friendly title company will do this for you, if you can't spare the time or don't know how to go about it.)

If you don't record your interest in the property, an unscrupulous owner might sell the property out from under you, or lease it to someone else, or take out another mortgage on it.

5. Make your payment into a neutral depository such as a bank or escrow company, and have them make the payments to the owner.

6. Whoever is buying from you (on the contract for

deed or whatever it is called in your state) must sign a quit-claim deed and put it into the escrow, to be delivered to you if he is more than thirty days late on a payment. If he performs as agreed, the deed is returned to him when he takes title by paying off the balloon.

7. Put a heavy prepayment penalty (say 15 or 20 percent of the purchase price) on your buyer for early payment of his contract. You don't want him to pay off the loan years early because you'd lose all that interest. Sometimes a sophisticated buyer slips in the words "or more" after the amount of the monthly payment. This sounds generous, but it gives him the automatic right to prepay the note at any time. So be sure to look for those words. If you find these, have him strike them out, and both of you initial the changes.

8. If title insurance is available in your state, you may want to get it. This insures that the seller really owns the property and that there aren't any hidden liens or mortgages against it. For much less money, a preliminary report can tell you virtually the same thing. It just doesn't provide any insurance. Use whichever level of certainty makes you comfortable.

A College Tuition Plan That Works

Forget all the plans your life-insurance salesman brings in the door. These plans are all tied to future dollars and they don't work! By the time your child grows up, the tuition will be far higher than the insurance can pay for.

Say we have a three-year-old child who will need a college education. We'll have to start paying for it fifteen years from now. What will that college education cost when the bills come in? It's hard to say, but we can be sure it will be several times more than it costs now.

Let's say we want $100,000 set aside for the child. That should leave some money left over.

All right, instead of buying insurance or an annuity

let's buy a $50,000 rental house or condo for no down payment. Let's arrange a fifteen-year mortgage on that house. The monthly payment will only be about 12 percent more than if we mortgaged it for thirty years, but our total interest payments will be far less.

Now let's rent the house to a tenant. And relax.

We'll let the tenant or tenants sit there for fifteen years and pay that house off free and clear by making all the payments for us. We just take the rent and turn it over to the mortgage holder.

Now it's fifteen years later. We own a house free and clear. What's a $50,000 house going to be worth fifteen years from now? Would $100,000 be a reasonable figure? Yes, indeed. It should be worth much more than that in high-growth parts of the country.

At this point we have an eighteen-year-old offspring ready for college. Sell the house. There's the money for the college education.

What did you take out of the plan? One hundred thousand dollars. What did you pay into the plan? Virtually nothing! When you think about it, that's not a bad plan.

15

INSTANT
MONEY-MAKERS

By NOW, IF YOU'VE BEEN PAYING ATTENTION, YOU'VE stored up all the basic knowledge you need to succeed in real-estate investing.

But there's always more to learn, especially when you've progressed beyond the cash-poor stage. When you've acquired a string of properties, new possibilities open up. You can sit back and let the properties earn money for you, but the time will come when you've used up most of their depreciation write-off. At that point you should take cash out of them by refinancing, getting second or third mortgages on them, or selling. Then, with plenty of cash at your command, you'll need to know smart ways to use it. I'll give you some suggestions in this chapter.

Having become a seller, you'll find yourself with a bundle of mortgages in your safe-deposit box. Through lack of knowledge, many investors keep these mortgages for years and let them pay themselves off. There are better things to do with real-estate paper. That's another area I'll cover in this chapter.

People build wealth with good ideas and hard work. In real estate the supply of good ideas is endless. Don't limit yourself to those in this chapter. Use your own mind. The more you use it, the better it will become at generating additional ideas for quickly increasing your wealth.

Ideas I've never heard of will occur to you. Every time you think of one, *write it down* and add it to this list. You won't forget it that way. You'll be like a snowball rolling downhill, getting bigger (and wealthier) as you collect ideas (and money) like snow along the way.

Creative Ways to Use Cash

First let's think for a moment about what you *don't* do with cash.

You don't pay retail for real estate and use cash for a down payment. Never pay in cash if you can't get a discount.

Likewise, you don't deal out cash to make up a short-fall in rental income from your properties. There are ways to eliminate negative cash flow, as you know from Chapter 11. And if your cash flow does turn negative for a month or two in spite of anything you can do, use OPM (other people's money) instead of your own to meet the extra expenses. Chapters 8, 9 and 10 showed you plenty of ways to beat the high cost of borrowing.

The only real reason for putting in a lot of cash is to get a discount. If I'm going to pay all cash, I want a 20 percent discount. Here are other ways to use your cash to increase your wealth.

1. Buy notes at discount and use them at face value.

Start buying existing real-estate mortgages for a large discount. You can find private lenders willing to sell their paper. Look in the classified column or run your own ad there.

You only want to buy mortgages (paper) that you can get for about fifty cents on the dollar. Look for mortgages that have lower interest rates than lenders are charging now, and that have a few years to run.

Keep buying until you have, say, $50,000 in paper for which you paid $25,000 in cash. Next, find a motivated seller with a $50,000 home or condo free and clear. Offer him $50,000 in paper for his property. (If he says no, don't take it personally. Just hunt up more sellers until one says yes.) You now have a $50,000 house free and clear.

Refinance this house (80 percent new loan) and take out $40,000 in cash. So now you have $40,000 in cash and $10,000 in equity. Take the $40,000 (grown from the $25,000 you started with, remember?) and buy more paper. Create a note for your $10,000 equity and offer that for a down payment also. By repeating this process over and over, you can build a large estate for yourself.

2. Buy with no interest.

We've all seen ads in recent years that read "Five Years No Interest." This kind of ad is placed by a builder trying to unload houses he is having a hard time selling (for a multitude of reasons).

He accepts a large down payment and lets you pay the balance during five years, in 60 equal equity payments and no interest. Let's take an example:

You buy a $70,000 house for $30,000 down and the balance paid in 60 monthly payments of $833.33.

In five years you own the house free and clear. By then you can be collecting more than $1,000 per month in rent. With no more payments to make, it all goes in your pocket. New homes need almost no maintenance. After five years you could:

(A) collect the income on however many homes you could afford to buy;

(B) refinance each home. Assuming 10 percent per year simple appreciation, the $70,000 home should be worth $105,000. An 80 percent new loan would be $84,000 cash in your pocket, tax-free (no income tax on borrowed money).

You could keep raising the rent every year and refinance every time, and your current rent would cover the payment on the new loan. Do it for as long as you live, and you won't pay any income tax on all that cash (as long as you never sell)!

3. Save interest by getting a shorter mortgage.

The 30-year fixed-interest amortized mortgage has been the standard form of home loan ever since the demise of the old-time interest-only mortgages in the Great Depression. Most borrowers don't realize what huge amounts of interest they pay over the term of the loan. With just a little extra cash, you can save yourself as much as $100,000 when you buy a house. All you have to do is get a 15-year amortized loan instead of a 30-year amortized loan. Let's analyze an actual example.

Buying a $100,000 home at 13 percent interest, the monthly payment on a 30-year loan is $1,106.20. The total payments: $1,106.20 × 12 months × 30 years = $398,232 or $298,232 in interest ($100,000 paid off the principal).

Buying the same $100,000 home at the same 13 percent interest, the monthly payment on a 15-year loan is $1,265.30. So the total payments are: $1,265.30 × 12 months × 15 years = $227,754 or $127,754 in interest.

Let's look at your benefit:

Difference in payment: $1,265.30
                       − 1,106.20
                       _____
                          159.10   more per month

Interest saved: $298,232
                        − 127,754
                        _____
                          170,478

Isn't that interesting! By paying $159.10 more per month, you can save $170,478 in interest charges! No wonder lenders prefer 30-year loans. And people, through lack of knowledge, just accept them.

With myself as an actual example (on a larger home) I saved $591,000 worth of interest with a $500 per month higher payment. The higher the price of the home, the more you save in interest.

4. The following is a fairly foolproof way to circum-

vent the due on sale clause in your mortgage. Put your house into a trust. In some states, such as Illinois, a land trust is used. Make your attorney the trustee. Make yourself the beneficiary. The trustee merely holds title for you and nothing else. When you want to sell the house and have the new owner keep the old loan, just change the name of the beneficiary to the new owner.

Let's look at the fire-insurance policy. The way a lender tells when a house has been sold is the name changes on the fire insurance policy. (If you were a new owner you wouldn't want the old owner to be paid if the house burned down, would you?) With the trust, the trustee can be named as the insured. When the "sale" takes place, the beneficiary's name is changed, but the policy is still in the name of the trustee (the attorney). The savings and loan will never know it happened.

If you ask your lender about it he'll say it won't work (he wishes it didn't). Can the lender exercise the due on sale clause when you put your property into a trust? No! The Garn-St. Germain law won't let him, if it's a Federal institution. You have effectively run around the due on sale clause.

Strategies for Sellers

As I mentioned at the beginning of this chapter, a time may come when you're ready to sell some of your properties. At that time, review Chapters 6, 8 and 11. They describe the techniques used to buy. Now you may need to help others buy. Why not turn these same techniques around and suggest them to some of your prospective purchasers?

Do you know how to pick up a few thousand dollars extra when you sell an apartment building? Look back to Chapter 8 and review idea number 16—for closing your purchase on the first or second of the month and thereby getting credit for the month's rents (which are paid in advance). Now, as a seller, you can reverse the procedure. Make the closing date near the *end* of the month, so that the month's rents go to you instead of to the buyer. If the building has ten units renting at $400 each, this would put $4,000 additional cash in your pocket.

What to Do with Paper

Now about that bundle of mortgages I mentioned early in this chapter.

As you've sold properties, you probably had to help the buyers by taking back a mortgage. Instead of passively sitting there and collecting the monthly payments, start to think in terms of your paper making you money. There are many, many things an investor can do with a mortgage. Here are a half-dozen.

1. Sell the note.

This is my least favorite. The problem is that you have to take a discount to get cash. If it's a low-interest and long-term note, you may have to take a 50 percent discount. For market interest rates and short term (two or three years) you can do much better. You will still lose around 20 cents on the dollar. Even if you need cash desperately, let's look at some other options.

2. Sell the payments.

That's probably something you haven't thought about. Yet it's done all the time. It's a simple way to raise cash. Let's take an example.

A mortgage pays $500 per month for three years (36 months). You would take in $500 × 36—$18,000. You might sell that for anywhere from $10,000 to $12,000 instant cash. The benefit here is you can raise cash while only discounting a small amount (the payments) instead of discounting a much larger amount (the mortgage itself).

3. Sell part interest in the mortgage.

You might sell about a one-fourth interest instead of

all, to raise cash. This will greatly reduce the amount of discount you have to take.

4. Pledge the mortgage as collateral.

Get to the bank, offer the note to back up a loan, and borrow any cash you might need.

5. Offer a mortgage on a mortgage.

Back in Chapter 8, the ninth of my 22 ways to buy with little cash was to offer mortgages (undiscounted) as a down payment on another piece of property. It lets you buy real estate at today's prices and get immediate benefits instead of waiting years for the mortgage to be paid off. However, this has tax disadvantages.

In the eyes of the IRS, when you signed over your mortgage as a down payment, you "used" it, so the income tax is due just as if you had collected payments over a period of years. Since that cash hasn't come to you yet, you might be short of money to pay the tax on it.

Here's a way to avoid the tax problem. Offer the seller, in lieu of a down payment, a mortgage on your mortgage! You can put a mortgage on anything. The original mortgage is the collateral for the mortgage you created. The difference is, the mortgage you were holding hasn't been "used." And the tax you'll have to pay can be spread over the life of the mortgage: *years,* instead of having to be paid in a lump sum.

A Thousand-Dollar Sentence

As you liquidate your older properties you'll probably buy newer ones (unless you've decided to retire, which you never need to do unless you feel like it). When you're buying a rental house, here's a way to pick up an extra thousand or so just by adding a sentence to your offer form.

When most people buy a house, they must wait as long as two or three months before they can get a tenant and start collecting rent. That's because the normal process goes like this: They write an offer; the offer is accepted. Six to eight weeks later they have a closing. Next day they run an ad for a tenant. Six to eight weeks after that, they rent the house.

But suppose you add one sentence to your offer form:

"Buyer reserves the right to show house to prospective tenants before closing."

Now let's see what happens. You write an offer. The offer is accepted. The very next day you run an ad for a tenant. You rent the house (before the closing). You may get the first month's rent from the tenant, and maybe a deposit too. This money can pay your closing costs. Then you close, the tenant moves in next day, and you have no lost rent.

An Interest-Free Loan for 18 Months

In Chapter 8, idea 22 for low-cash buying was to use a split-funding down payment (half now, half in 12 to 18 months, say). But there are two ways to write the offer. One of those two contains hidden profit for you.

Let's analyze two different split-funding offers on the same property.

Offer A: $100,000 price, $10,000 down, $90,000 mortgage to be carried by seller at 12 percent interest. Payments of $1,000 per month until paid. $10,000 payment in additional principal to be paid 18 months after closing.

Offer B: $100,000 price, $20,000 down payment, to be paid $10,000 at closing and $10,000 18 months after closing. $80,000 mortgage to be carried by seller at 12 percent interest, payment of $1,000 per month until paid.

Even though they appear to be basically the same, there is a major difference in the two offers. In Offer A you pay interest on the second payment of $10,000. This interest totals $1,800 out of your pocket over 18 months.

In Offer B you pay *no* interest on the second $10,000.

In effect, you have received an interest-free loan of $10,000 for a year and a half.

So, whenever you make an offer for a split down payment, always write it in the form of Offer B. You'll be amazed at how many times it is accepted. Seller's agents (broker, attorneys and the like) just don't catch it. If it is noticed, use it as a bargaining point: "Well, if I agree to pay interest on the $10,000 will you do . . ."

The Power of the Rent Raise

Throughout this book I've been advising you not to buy property for quick turnover. Here's an exception to that advice. I want to include it because some of you reading this book have no idea how much profit you can make by a simple rent raise.

Ten percent or more of the buildings out there are charging under-market rents for a variety of reasons. There are owners with lack of knowledge, owners living in their buildings (they fall in love with tenants), owners fearful of vacancies (not realizing that tenants would rather pay more rent than go to the expense of moving to pay the higher rent somewhere else), and so on.

Here's how you can take advantage of such situations. The key fact is the potential profits to be made from a simple 10 percent rent raise. Let's take a ten-unit building. Rents are $300 a month. The building will sell for eight times the gross income. So here's how the current selling price would work out:

$300/month × 10 units × 12 months × 8 (gross multiplier) = $288,000 sales price.

You know from researching the area that this building's rents are 10 percent under market. If you take over the building and raise the rents, you can resell it for a fast profit.

Remember the lease-option technique I described in Chapter 14? Use it now. Acquire a lease with option to buy the property and offer (listen, now!) to manage the property *free* during the lease period. That's so you'll be the person, as manager, to collect and raise rents.

And that's what you do. As soon as you are manager, you raise the rents 10 percent, which is $30 a month. Now let's see what the building is worth:

$330/month × 10 units × 12 months × 8 = $316,800 sales price.

You can get title by exercising your option at any time. When you have found a buyer, exercise it and buy the building, then sell it for the new price.

By running a simultaneous closing, you can use the new buyer's money for any down-payment requirements, and you walk away with the difference in price. That difference is $316,000 minus $288,000 = $28,000. Take your profit in cash, paper, whatever you can get.

Just repeat the process wherever you find a building with below-market rents. If you can get an option for a few thousand and make $28,000 (less closing costs), it won't take you many turnovers to get wealthy. Besides, if you offer to manage the building for free for up to one year, owners should give you a break on the option price. What could you make if you found a building where rents were $50 to $75 under market? Exciting, isn't it?

16

HOW TO GET A LARGE DISCOUNT FROM A SELLER

AN OWNER GLADLY KNOCKS 18 PERCENT OFF HIS ASKING price without any concessions from you?

Yes. It's perfectly possible in certain situations. It happens often.

And I'm not talking about situations where the owner has overpriced his house for negotiating purposes.

By learning to recognize these special situations, and knowing how to convince the owner that he isn't sacrificing anything by giving you a discount, you can do both parties a big favor. This is one of the profit strategies you won't learn in school, not even business school. And it's so potent I think it deserves a mini-chapter to itself.

When It Will Work

The method works on houses commonly known to real-estate people as FSBO (For Sale by Owner) houses. One in every twelve homes is sold this way.

Since you must deal directly with the owner, his property must not have an active "Exclusive Right to Sell" listing with an agent. In rare cases the method will appeal to an owner (a smart, experienced one) who's just beginning to think of selling and hasn't talked to real-estate agents yet—or who may want to see how he can do without one. But the discouraged seller is the best prospect.

If the property was listed, didn't sell, and the listing has expired, the situation is made to order for you.

However, take warning: If you were shown the property through a broker, and you buy the property after the listing has expired, the broker may retain his right to claim a commission for several months afterward. Read the listing contract. It will tell you.

First of all, you should understand the one big fact that makes this method attractive to sellers: When someone sells a house in the usual way, he has to pay a variety of imaginative one-time fees such as closing costs, loan points (on FHA new financing), commissions, appraisal charges, (sometimes) title insurance premiums (depending on custom), legal expenses, etc. These come out of the money the buyer hands over before the seller receives it (or the seller may have to pay some himself, thereby reducing his profit). So there's a gap of thousands of dollars between the listed, agreed-on price of the house and the true net to the seller. Some sellers know this sad fact. Many don't.

The Art of Asking for a Discount

If you begin by asking a seller to knock down his price 18 percent or so, he may kill you nine different ways. Or he may bust out laughing. There's a much better way to begin.

The basic question you should ask the seller over the phone is a fairly innocent one: "Mr. Seller, would you sell the property with FHA financing through a broker?"

You're hoping for an answer that will approximate one of the following:

"Yes I would."

"Yes, we listed it that way." (A very encouraging answer.)

"I don't see why not."

In other words, a positive response. He may not realize it, but a seller who answers that way has told you he will sell you the house at a discount.

So then you sit down with him and explain the net he will receive if he sells FHA through a broker.

Four Big Subtractions

With pencil and paper, you and he work out the following arithmetic.

Price:	$50,000	
Minus 5%	2,500	(homes normally sell for 5–7 percent below listed price)
Leaves	47,500	
Minus 6%	3,000	(broker's commission)*
Leaves	44,500	
Minus 5%	2,500	(FHA points. One point = 1 percent)†
Leaves	42,000	
Minus	1,000	(closing costs)
Leaves	41,000	

"Mr. Seller, that would be your net if you sold the property FHA through a broker. And that's the price I will pay you for your property." To make this even more effective, offer a quick close.

Your discount off the listed price is $9,000 divided by $50,000. That's an 18 percent discount.

This reasoning is fairly simple. However, you may need a little practice in talking with sellers before you

* Brokerage commissions vary. Use the prevailing rate in your area. Usually it is between 5 and 7 percent.
† FHA points vary too, from year to year. Almost any broker can tell you the current rate. You should use the current rate in your negotiations.

Note that your calculations are all based on the $50,000 figure (more profit for you).

can explain it easily. This is called work. The harder you work, the luckier you get, and the more property you acquire.

Handling the Balance

On a transaction like the above, let's see how you would pay for the house after buying it.

You offered $41,000, which was accepted. The existing loan, we'll say, is an older FHA fully assumable loan for $30,000 at 9 percent interest. The payments on it are $241.40 a month. These will be coming out of your pocket from now on.

You pay the seller $500 down on the $11,000 balance. He carries back (allows you to owe him) the other $10,500 on a 15-year loan at 10 percent, which figures out to monthly payments of $112.85. (Remember, we're dealing with motivated sellers.)

So the $241.40 (old loan) plus $112.85 (seller's second mortgage) makes a total of $354.25 per month you'll be paying for a house priced at $50,000.

As in all the examples through the book, you've made an investment for a very low down payment and a reasonable monthly charge. The seller will get just as much as he would have received selling the property through a broker with FHA financing. Also, he will avoid a bunch of red tape and delays.

There will still be some closing costs involved of perhaps a few hundred dollars.

17

INVESTORS SHOULDN'T MANAGE THEIR PROPERTY, BUT—

"He is the rich man who can avail himself of all men's faculties."
—Ralph Waldo Emerson

I COULD WRITE THIS CHAPTER IN JUST THREE WORDS: Don't do it! Why not manage your property? One reason: because you're probably working for a living right now, which means you have a limited amount of time to devote to creating wealth on the side. Ten hours a week is probably going to be the most time you can spend on it.

The Management Problem

If you yourself manage your property you'll run head-on into this problem by the time you own three or four properties, even small ones. You'll find yourself spending ten hours a week on management and *no* hours on acquiring more properties.

You'll be fixing faucets and toilets, collecting rents, shopping for light bulbs and lawn seed, writing checks for paint and tile and glass, maybe talking with prospective new tenants.

At that point your financial independence program grinds to a halt. You are locked into a low-profit, time-consuming enterprise.

Keep in mind how wealth is built: by getting the maximum return for your time. If you want to make $10 an hour, swing a paint brush. If you want to make $300 or $400 an hour, write offers!

Keep yourself out of the management process and in the acquisition process. How? Buy a management package instead of doing it yourself.

In other words, hire a part-time manager. This is simpler than it sounds.

When you own a few small properties you don't need a full-time manager. You need a firm of property managers. It can do all the chores of looking after your properties in only a few hours a week, because it combines the management of numerous properties. It takes advantage of what efficiency experts call "economies of scale." In other words, it gets the benefits of wholesale over retail. It knows all the time-saving, money-saving, effort-saving angles. A good property-management firm takes care of repairs, maintenance, collecting rents, filling vacancies, keeping records and practically everything else that's needed. You won't have to go near your properties.

How to Find a Management Firm

Look in the Yellow Pages of your phone book under the section headed Real Estate Management. In a major city this section will fill several pages.

But keep in mind that all the managers listed won't be equally good. In most states, any licensed real-estate broker can call himself a property manager even if he or she has no experience, expertise or aptitude.

So you can't quite pick blindfolded—but you almost can. Just look for listed firms that carry the initials CPM or AMO after their names.

CPM stands for Certified Property Manager; AMO stands for Accredited Management Organization. No firm is entitled to use those initials unless it has passed certain tests and is continuously meeting established standards. So you're reasonably assured of getting competent management when you deal with one of these firms.

That doesn't mean never deal with anyone else. But if you do, find a firm or a manager who is personally recommended by someone you know. For example, when you get acquainted with other property owners by joining your local Apartment Owners' Association (a tax-deductible expense) you'll find some who are well satisfied with someone small and local who hasn't yet earned the CPM or AMO. In that case the management fee may be smaller.

Another way to find a good firm is to visit the offices of a few. Ask the manager for names of owners whose properties he is currently managing. Then phone some of those owners and ask if they would recommend the firm. All this takes a little time, but it's certainly better than going in blind.

How Much Should You Pay?

Guess what? Fees are negotiable!

You'll probably be quoted fees running from 3 to 4 percent of the gross income for a very large apartment building up to 10 percent for a one-family home. You can get this quotation scaled down if you implant in the manager's mind that you're going to be a major investor—even if you've just bought your first investment home.

Here's one way to do it. Ask the property manager, "What will you charge me to run ten rental homes in this area?" Wait for the answer. Then say, "Fine. I just closed on my first house, and I'll give them to you just as fast as I can close."

When he hears this, he'll probably rear back and demand more. So you compromise. Suggest a sliding scale. If you pay 10 percent of the gross rental for one house, you'll pay 9 percent for two houses, 8 percent for three, down to a minimum of 5 percent for six houses or more.

Remember: If you don't ask, you'll never receive!

If You Must Manage, Get Good Tenants

In spite of what I've said, some of you reading this book will still feel that you can't afford even a part-time manager—that you must do the managing yourself for a while, due to high prices or low rents or both. Okay. That's understandable. If you're going to run your own rentals, let me give you some guidelines. They served me well when I was starting out, and they serve other people well today.

First, four rules for selecting tenants.

Begin by looking at the family's income. Of course, you ask for this information on the rental application. If the rent exceeds 30 percent of their income, you'll have trouble collecting because they can't afford it. You'd better turn them away.

Even if their income seems high enough, according to the application, verify it. Make sure their job(s) and income(s) are truthfully reported by calling their employers.

And if they've just started new jobs, find out who their previous employers were and how long they worked there. You don't want job-hoppers. They may move out of your house or apartment soon after they move in.

Even if a family has passed the income test, don't rent to them immediately. There are three other important steps in qualifying them as desirable residents.

Run a credit check on them (about a $10 fee). People who have a history of paying their bills will probably pay the rent.

You have access to credit checks if you're a member of an Apartment Owners' Association. If not, look under Credit Reporting Agencies in the Yellow Pages, and phone them for quotes. Credit chains like TRW are national in scope.

The third step is to check with the landlord from whom an applicant previously rented.

Notice I said "previously rented," not "currently renting." The current landlord may say anything to get the tenant out. But the previous landlord has no reason to lie. He'll give you straight facts. This is why your rental application form should include a blank for "name and address of previous landlord" as well as one for the present landlord. Be sure the applicant fills in that first blank. You may not bother asking about the present landlord, but you should *always* get in touch with the previous one.

If someone looks okay after these first three checkups, there is still a final test to make sure the family is the kind you want.

Stop by, unannounced, at the family's present residence. Invent a reason, of course. Find something on the rental application about which you have a question. After you have been there a few minutes, ask to use the bathroom. On the way out, glance into the bedrooms. Get a good idea how the family lives day to day, and you'll know how your rental property is likely to be treated.

Seven More Tips for Management

1. If you own an apartment building, apply one other test to applicants: Don't rent to them if you dislike them when you first meet them. Your other tenants won't like them either. In fact, long-time tenants might move to get away from them. One rotten apple can empty your building. So be careful to keep disagreeable people out, even though their income and credit standing are great. You're better off staying vacant another week or two in order to rent to someone pleasant.

2. If you do get bad tenants, offer to buy them out.

Few managers ever think of this. Yet it's the easiest (and usually quickest and cheapest) way to get someone out.

"I'll give you a month's rent if you vacate within three days." Sounds expensive? It's not. Just consider:

For a $400 cash payment (if that's the rent), you can get the vacancy you want in three days. You may fill that vacancy with someone desirable in a couple of weeks or less (which you obviously couldn't do if the undesirables were still there).

And consider the costs of the usual alternative, which is evicting the tenants legally. In some states this might cost $1,000 or $2,000 in attorney's fees, court costs and assorted other expenses. The eviction procedure might take several months. Wouldn't you rather be collecting rent from some new occupant during those months? Aren't the savings, and the extra income, worth $400 or so?

3. Smile whenever you are talking on the telephone. This will automatically take any gruffness out of your voice, and let you come across as pleasant.

4. Raise your rents a little above what you need—but offer a discount for prompt payment. The chance to save some money is a powerful inducement to pay the rent on time. (For more on this subject, see Chapter 19 on coping with rent control.)

5. If you have difficulty filling vacancies, offer rewards to your present tenants for bringing in new tenants (rewards to be paid when the new tenants move in). Post "Reward" offers in the laundry room, on bulletin boards, etc. Try a $100 reward. It's just a fraction of a month's rent and is a tax-deductible business expense.

6. If you still have a problem with vacancies, look for a need in your community and fill it. Is there a specific group of people who are having trouble finding lodging? Appealing to them—and maybe offering them some special service—can cure a large vacancy factor in a hurry, at above-market rents.

Look in the "Apartments for Rent" newspaper columns. Look not for what's there, but for what *isn't* there.

For instance, maybe there aren't any ads headed "Divorcees Only." Why don't you try one? Under the two-word heading you might add a line: "You must have at least one child." Then you might turn one of your units into a playroom, or perhaps provide a baby-sitting service in a nearby building. You can charge for this, of course.

Look and see if there are ads for "Cat Owners Only." If not, this is another good bet, because many apartment managers won't allow pets. Just limit your offer to owners of neutered or spayed cats only: this will diminish their love-yowling. And be sure to take a large pet deposit to cover the damage that cats can do to drapes, rugs and furnishings.

A simpler idea, if other apartment owners aren't advertising it, is to offer rentals to "Retired Only." This will give you a quiet building and harmonious tenants. As an extra attraction you might buy a van (tax-deductible) and provide a shuttle to the nearby shopping center for tenants without cars.

To sum up my point about filling unmet needs: If you'll invest money to give a special group of prospects something extra, you can get back many times what you pay out. At the same time you can eliminate vacancies and build a waiting list.

7. If your apartment building is always full, something is wrong!

A full apartment building is generally a sign of poor management. Why? Because it almost always means the rents are *too low*.

To strive for a full building is human nature. But this won't maximize your income. Several years ago a large management firm ran a computer study that proved this point—at least for larger buildings, on which the study was based. The firm wanted to know what vacancy factor produced the highest total income. The study showed that income for each building became maximum when rents were high enough so that 15 percent of the units were usually vacant. (If you set rents so high that you can rent only 85 percent of the units, you've reached what economists call "the point of diminishing returns.")

See the point? Raise your rents until you incur vacancies. Then your income will be larger than if you kept the building full at lower rents.

As Manager, Should You Live in the Building?

Here is a sort of corollary to the previous point:

8. The cardinal sin for an owner is living in a building while managing it. Never do this.

Maybe you think you can manage easier if you live on the premises. I doubt this (I'll tell you why in a minute). But even if it happens to be true in your case, your profits will be less. The trouble is, you're human. Some, maybe most, of your tenants will get to be your personal friends. They will be Jack and Joan instead of Mr. and Mrs. Smith. You can't raise Jack and Joan's rent because they've told you ten reasons why they can't afford it, and you've taken this to heart.

Show me a building where the owner has lived for five years, and I'll show you a building where the rents are two years or more behind the going rates.

But here's the other reason why an owner shouldn't be the resident manager. Some tenants will stop you with a complaint or request every time they see you. Or they'll come knocking on your door. Or they'll phone, because you're right upstairs and can get their windows cleaned right now.

A manager who doesn't own the place can tell tenants, "The owners won't let me do that," or "The owners can't afford it." But it's much harder for you as owner-manager to say "I can't afford it," especially if you obviously lead a rather luxurious life.

If you'd like to get a good overall idea of the problems of apartment managers, drop in at the public library and look up *The New Yorker* magazine for October 24, 1983. It contains a long article about the Brennan brothers, who are noted as managers of some of the biggest and most successful apartment buildings in New York City. The article described many complaints the Brennans hear every day, and I'll quote just a few:

> *Tales Managers Tell*
>
> "The funny thing about a complainer," George Brennan said, "is that when the building's spotless they want to know why we didn't clean the sewers, why aren't we doing the Sanitation Department's work, how come the sidewalk's dirty?"
>
> "I got an emergency call at 2 A.M.," Pete Brennan said. "A lady says get up here right away. I put on some pants and go up there. Guess what it is? You'll never guess. A roach on the floor. Dead. She couldn't sleep with it there. That's the emergency. I had to pick it up and flush it for her."
>
> George said, "A lady called and said the floor was dirty. The manager said, 'I don't know how that could be, I was just up on your floor and the carpet looked spotless.' She says, 'Well, it's not *dirty* dirty but I didn't hear the vacuum!' "

If you're ready for these kinds of stresses, surprises and botherations, go right ahead. Move into a building and manage it!

When you finally can afford at least a part-time manager, and have signed one up, here's one last bit of important advice:

Motivate your manager. Offer him a financial arrangement that will put more money in his pocket when he increases the building's income.

You might say something like "This building is now grossing $5,000 a month. I'll give you a percentage (to be negotiated) of every dollar it grosses above that amount."

This means he can count on raises based on performance. So you'll find your rents keeping up with the current market level. And your vacancies will be rented more quickly.

18

THE TAX MAN COMETH! SO WHAT?

WHILE YOU'RE BUILDING WEALTH (AND AFTER YOU'RE wealthy) the problem is to stay that way.

The 1986 tax law will go a long way toward helping. We will be able to keep a lot more of our money, both while we're making it and after it's made. After the transition period of 1987 (during which there will be four tax brackets ranging from 15 percent to 38.5 percent), we will be paying (from 1988 on) taxes in only two brackets, 15 percent and 28 percent. Although most Americans won't be affected, there will also be a 5 percent surcharge on the higher levels of taxable income. This will have the effect of imposing a third rate of 33 percent, and is brought about by a phasing out of the 15 percent rate on the lower portion of income and loss of the personal exemption.

The benefits of depreciation have also been greatly altered in two major areas:

1. The 19-year straight-line and accelerated depreciation has been removed for real estate. Depreciation is now 27½ years for residential property and 31½ years for all other real estate.

2. Depreciation may no longer be used to offset income from salaries, portfolio income (dividends, royalties, and interest), or active business income. There is one exception, however. On real-estate rental activities in which you actively participate, you may offset other

income by declaring losses (using the new depreciation schedule) of up to $25,000. This amount will phase out as income reaches $100,000; however, most of you reading this book don't have that lovely problem.

Real-estate losses in excess of the above allowable deductions will be treated as a passive investment loss. It cannot be used to offset other income (except from real estate); however, it can be deferred until there is income from passive investments, and then be used to offset them until such time as the investment generating the loss has been disposed of.

These limitations apply to investments purchased after December 31, 1986. Any investments made prior to this date will have losses phased out on a sliding scale, as follows:

> 1987—65% allowed
> 1988—40% allowed
> 1989—20% allowed
> 1990—10% allowed
> 1991—(and after) no passive losses allowed

The Trouble with Selling

Let's say you've reached the point where you own several properties. They've gone up in value. Brokers and buyers are interested in them. Naturally you're tempted to sell and pocket a nice profit.

I know you keep hearing that real-estate investors should buy-sell, buy-sell. That makes a nice living for brokers. But for you there are two problems with selling real estate:

1. You convert yourself back into dollars, which are a depreciating asset.

2. You'll start to run to the bank with your dollars and you won't make it. That tall guy in the red, white

and blue suit will be in your way, grabbing your arm. On April 15 you'll have to hand him the income tax.

How About Swapping?

When you have a piece of property that you want to get rid of, instead of selling it think about trading or exchanging it for another piece of property. You can find brokers who specialize in arranging two-way or three-way or even multiparty exchanges. They'll help you "trade up"—get property that's worth as much as the increased value of your own property.

When you swap, a wonderful thing happens to you. You've gotten rid of your property, you've become richer, but the tax is postponed indefinitely or forever. You're way ahead of where you'd be if you sold the same property you are exchanging, paid tax on the profit, and then bought another property with the cash left over.

Or Refinancing?

Let's discuss a different way of investing. Let's say Peter Profit is thirty years old when he buys a single-family house to use as a rental. It's worth $75,000. And let's say Peter will live to be eighty.

Every year Peter raises his rent. In six or seven years he waits for a good money market, then refinances his house. He takes out, say, $40,000 in cash, which he'll never need to pay (the tenant will pay it back for him). The increased rent flow will take care of the higher payments on the new mortgage. The house is worth about $125,000.

Peter keeps raising the rent every year. In six or seven more years, he refinances again and takes out another $80,000 or $90,000. In six or seven more years he takes out $160,000 to $175,000. At the end of forty or fifty years, Peter may have taken over a half million dollars out of a single-family home, and he hasn't paid a dime in income tax, because a refinance is not a taxable event. A *sale* is a taxable event.

Leaving Your Family Wealthy

But wait, there's more. Here's the best part. After Peter dies, the IRS forgives the income tax he would have paid if the house is sold. It's a tough way to get forgiven, but we all have to think about it. If you and I don't do estate planning, in a few years from now if something happens to one of us, the surviving spouse and child could owe tens of thousands in inheritance tax that they shouldn't have to pay.

Your estate (especially your real estate) can be set up so the rest of the family doesn't get hammered by the tax collector after you've gone. The combination of estate-tax exemptions created by the 1981 tax law and some other arrangements, such as writing your will in certain ways, can greatly reduce what the family pays. That's a nice little feeling for you during the rest of your life. So be sure to talk to a tax specialist about it. If Peter's children or other heirs decide to keep the old house and rent it to a tenant, they take its present value and start to depreciate it so they can avoid tax on the rental income. And they can take out money tax-free by refinancing as Peter did.

Expanding the Peter Profit example, imagine if you bought one rental house a year for seven years, and then refinanced one year after year. You could use the money to live like a king.

Why Do I Have to Sell?

You may have heard that you *have* to sell, or it's wise to sell, a property after six or seven years. Here's the thought process behind it. Let's look at our formula again: Cash Flow + Equity Buildup − Depreciation = Taxable Income.

On a loan that's amortized normally, your buildup of equity during the first five years is small. After five years, a larger part of each loan payment goes to pay off the principal, thereby building up your equity.

Also, your cash flow gets higher as you raise your rents year after year. Look at the formula once more. As your equity buildup grows, it washes out your depreciation, so your cash flow becomes positive instead of negative. Then you owe income tax on cash you're taking in.

One solution is selling. That's the standard solution, taught to most investors. But to repeat, there are two problems with selling: You pay tax, and you convert yourself to dollars which go down in value.

A better solution is to refinance. You need only a loose money market (low interest rates), and the rents should be high enough (you've been raising them for six to eight years) to cover the higher loan payments.

After you've refinanced, your cash flow and equity buildup are small again, and the formula works to your advantage. Best of all, the refinance puts tens of thousands of dollars in your bank account—and you owe no tax on those dollars. The government doesn't charge income tax on *borrowed* money, only on *earned* money.

Take These Off!

So much for depreciation, the key to a tax-free life. Now let's look at other tax angles you should keep in mind.

All your expenses in finding, maintaining, renting and selling properties (except your own home) are deductible from income of the property. If you attend an investment seminar or lecture or educational course, write off the tuition fees. If you stay at a hotel while you're attending any of these, or while you're negotiating for property, write off the hotel bill and meals (80 percent) and your transportation back and forth. Same for transportation if you take trips to collect rent, and for the postage you pay.

If you subscribe to any publications or newsletters about real estate (or about other kinds of investments), write off the subscriptions. Write off the cost of any investment book you buy (including this one, naturally). Write off whatever you pay your CPA and your attorney in connection with real-estate investments.

If your property (including your home, this time) is damaged by fire, flood, storm, earthquake, explosion, vandalism, theft or "other casualty," you can deduct whatever loss isn't covered by insurance (it has to be over $100 if it's your own home, though). "Other casualty" means practically any sudden violent happening that causes damage—a car crashing into your property, a tree falling on it, a siege of smog that blisters the paint, a bursting pipe that floods floors and ruins rugs.

The catastrophe doesn't have to be major. If your underinsured roof happens to be torn away by one freakish gust of wind, you can claim a casualty deduction for your out-of-pocket costs not paid by the insurance company.

However, the IRS will reject your claim for creeping calamities like termites eating your house, or the bursting of a boiler that has been gradually going bad for a long time. (Even then, you could deduct damage to rugs and drapes, because what happened to them was sudden.)

Just keep in mind that a claim for casualty losses will set off an alarm at the IRS. If the loss is substantial, an IRS agent may soon be asking about it. He'll challenge your valuation if he can. Be ready to prove any casualty loss you deduct. If possible, take pictures before the damage is repaired.

In fact, it's a good idea to use up a roll of film in and

around your property every year or so. Take pictures of the furniture, draperies, shrubs, stairways and so on. Then you can produce before-and-after evidence of damage.

Even when you have no proof, you can deduct whatever you spend to repair or replace the damaged assets. Claim this as an ordinary expense, not a casualty loss.

Normally, casualty losses have to be charged against income you receive in the same year as the loss. But you may not have much income in a year when your property is wiped out in a major disaster like a hurricane or tornado. In places which the President has declared disaster areas (he did this in 24 states during a typical year), the tax man gives you the choice of claiming the casualty loss against income earned the previous year. To do this, have your CPA prepare an amended return on Form 1040. If you write "disaster-area loss" on the envelope, the IRS says it will give the return faster handling. Such losses are usually covered by insurance.

Be a Pack Rat

You will still be entitled to interest deductions on your investment property up to the extent of your investment income (the definitions of both of these terms have been expanded—check with your CPA). Remember, your mortgage payments are only partly interest. They're also partly reduction of the principal, which isn't deductible. Keep the bank's repayment schedule or other breakdown on hand, so you can prove to the tax man what part of each payment represented interest.

In fact you'd better keep every scrap of paper that may help you prove you're entitled to deductions. The IRS says the burden of proof is on you. You may have to prove that something happened or didn't happen. Proof usually is pieces of paper—receipts, bills, letters, letter documents, canceled checks, ledgers, cash books and the like.

The IRS may challenge a deduction years after you file the return, and papers would be too hard to round up then. Keep them as you go along. One way is to drop them into certain file folders immediately. Then put the folders in a safe place. Your desk drawer isn't safe enough. If the building burns down, you don't want all the papers that could establish your tax loss destroyed in the same fire. Important backup materials ought to be in a safe-deposit box at your bank, or in your accountant's office or in a fireproof file cabinet.

How long should you hold on to real-estate records? As long as your tax returns are "open" for tax audit. Usually the statute of limitations will close a tax return three years after the return was due, or two years after you paid it (whichever occurs later). But there is no statute of limitations on fraud, so why not keep all important proofs permanently, just in case?

Anyhow, hold onto records as long as you hold property covered by those records. If you sell the property, you'll need to be able to prove how much you paid for it, and how much you spent on improvements. If you sell a property you received by gift or inheritance, you may be asked to prove what the previous owner paid for it.

All this is just a simple matter of housekeeping and accounting. But some of you probably put together your records for your tax account around February or March or April. Why wait until then? When is the time to do income tax? December! If you see you have a tax problem in December, you can do something about it. Once the year ends, you're too late.

As one simple example, if you need a deduction, you can prepay your state income taxes in December so you can write it off your federal return in that year. You can also pay other bills in December even though they may not be due until later.

Don't Be Afraid of Audits

The wealthier you get, the more the chance the IRS will decide to audit your tax return. But also, the wealthier you get, the more experts you'll have working for you. With experts and good records, you've got nothing to fear.

People think the IRS is a nonprofit government agency. It is a money-making organization. To make money, an audit must uncover about $75 an hour in increased tax assessments. So how do you make yourself audit-proof? Don't let them think they can make $75 per hour from you.

The best way to do this is to have your return prepared by a really reputable firm, one you can work well with. Find out about the firm before you go to them. A bad preparer can get you audited. In fact, the IRS keeps a "problem preparer" list of firms, and audits all their returns.

A good firm probably won't let IRS auditors go near you. To begin with, it usually guarantees clients that if any penalty is assessed against a return due to errors in the preparation of the return, the firm itself will absorb this charge.

Even if it doesn't give you such a guarantee, a good firm prides itself in knowing how to cope with audits. So it will probably tell you, "Just sort out your records and give them to us. We'll decide what to show the IRS, and we'll do the talking. If it gets sticky, we may bring in your lawyer too—but you stay away."

If you're not sure about the expertise of an accounting firm, ask for the names of some of its other clients, and ask if you can check with them. Or find a good firm by going the other way around: Ask some of your richest and smartest friends who they use.

What's Been Kept

1. Once-in-a-lifetime exclusion on sale of your home (principal residence).

At age fifty-five or later, you get another tax-free privilege, but once only. When you sell your home, as much as $125,000 (it used to be $100,000) is completely free of tax. To qualify, you must have lived in the home three of the last five years.

To elect this one-time exclusion, attach a signed statement to your tax return. You must say you elect to take the exclusion, and you must include the following:

a) Cost at purchase
b) Date of purchase
c) Date of sale
d) Names of owners at sale, along with their social security numbers
e) How title is vested (form of ownership), joint tenancy, tenants in common, etc.
f) Length of any absences from the property (other than vacation) during the preceding five years
g) Any other elections under this provision taken by owners at the time of sale

Warning: This is a one-time exemption. You can't carry what's left. Older couples planning to marry should ask each other, "Have you used your home exemption?" It may save a lot of taxes if one of you sells a home before the marriage rather than later. Discuss this with your accountant *before* the wedding.

2. "Rollover" provision.

You can still sell your home and buy a new one within 24 months. You can defer all taxes as long as the price is the same or higher and your new mortgage is the same or higher. You must move into the new home within the 24-month period.

Warning: You can do this as often as you please, provided you don't do it twice within 24 months.

3. Estate and Gift Tax

The estate-tax provisions have been left intact. By 1987 you will be able to exempt $600,000 of your estate from tax (up from $500,000 in 1986). If your net worth is more than the above exemption, consult an estate-planning attorney. With proper planning, a married couple can exempt $1,200,000 from estate tax (1987 and beyond).

You can still give away $10,000 per year per person and not trigger gift tax. A major portion of your estate-tax bill can be avoided by doing this.

Example: Couple with 3 children

$20,000 to each child (husband/wife $10,000 each)
$60,000 for 3 children each year
$600,000 over 10 years
$1,200,000 over 20 years.

If you're working for a wage now, this may not seem applicable to you. However, in a few short years of real-estate investing, you can be a millionaire plus, and you'll be a candidate for estate planning.

19

WHAT TO DO ABOUT RENT CONTROL

RENT CONTROL IS THE GREAT FEAR OF ANYONE WHO owns apartments. Control means that local bureaucrats, rather than normal forces of supply and demand, determine how much rent he can charge. They may not allow him enough to cover rising costs.

Rent controls have been spreading in recent years. So fear is spreading too. However, much of the fear is unfounded.

If you're using the investment methods recommended in this book, you're looking at rental income and rent increases as your personal golden key to financial independence. But now you see this income threatened. What should you do?

1. Don't panic. Take a long hard look at rent controls. Learn what they are, why they come, what happens afterward, and what you can do about them.

2. Help educate your community about what will happen if they come. Join the political campaign and get out the vote. Renters think they have a lot to gain from controls, but they can be shown that it will put them in worse trouble later. Some communities really have voted against rent control.

3. If it looks as though rent control is coming regardless, take steps to protect yourself. Later in this chapter I'll show you how.

4. If you're under rent control, start a long-range pro-

gram (not a crash program) to dispose of your properties profitably. I'll get to this too.

What Causes Rent Control

Rent control is (or may be) brought about by housing shortages.

As long as there is a surplus of rental housing, landlords seldom try to raise rents above the going rates. If they do, people move out. But when vacant apartments get scarce, renters tend to go along with raises rather than move out. They know they may not find another place to live.

A city's normal vacancy factor is around 5 percent. When it drops to 2 percent and is still trending downward, rents climb automatically. Some renters begin to be priced out of the market and others feel a painful pinch. After a while angry groups storm City Hall, hollering "Do something."

In the past, supply would increase to meet demand. But apartment builders have held off lately because of the rises in land costs and building costs and borrowing charges. That's why rent controls have come to many municipalities.

A better answer to scarcity of rental units is to provide more units rather than freeze the rents. Get apartments built through incentives, low-interest bonds, whatever. Or maybe let owners raise rents and issue rental vouchers to low-income families to offset the increases. (In December 1983 Congress passed a $315 million experimental program along this line.)

But such action takes a lot of thrashing around by politicians and civil servants. It also takes time. Time passes slowly for people hunting places to live. So rent control is the quick response, likely to be voted in by renters if they're a majority. It sounds so easy. Just rein in the "greedy landlords" and there'll be no problem.

Clampdown and Consequences

But this quick fix doesn't work. Under rent control the problem gets worse as time passes. Ask the cities that have tried it. Here's what happens:

1. Housing deteriorates. Why? Because improvements, repairs and maintenance cost money. Nothing an owner might do to improve his rental units, or even keep them as good as they are, would increase his cash flow. He thinks, "No matter how bad my building gets, nobody will move." The profit margin keeps shrinking because he still has to pay taxes and debt service and other monthly expenses. So he spends the least he can, and his units gradually wear out. Tenants find themselves paying the same rent for poorer and poorer housing.

2. Housing gets scarcer. When there's a low ceiling on profits (or no chance for profits at all) nobody wants to build new units, and few investors want to buy old ones. They all say, "Hey, let's get out of here, and go where we can get a decent return on our money."

As buildings wear out, owners abandon them rather than keep on paying taxes and making repairs required by law. Urban decay sets in.

To see the end results of rent control, go to New York City. It tried controls as a temporary emergency measure in World War II and couldn't loosen them until 1970 because they subsidized millions of poverty-level voters. There are miles of empty or burnt-out buildings. In three years alone, from 1965 to 1968, about 100,000 housing units in New York were abandoned or burned for the fire insurance. Now there are many thousands of homeless New Yorkers (nobody knows how many) living in streets or subways or ruined buildings or charity shelters.

In demand areas (places where more people want to live) vacancy factors go to zero after rent control arrives. The older people there hang on to their apartments. Younger people who want to come into the area to work and live can't find housing. You can guess what this does to the local economy. A prime example is Santa Monica, California, which passed one of the nation's toughest rent-control ordinances. The population is tilting more and more heavily to low-income senior citizens. Some public schools have closed. Business isn't exactly booming.

These facts should be known. If you help, maybe your community can be convinced that rent control is ruinous. But as the 1980s move along and the rental shortage gets worse, more and more cities are sure to hear demands for control. Just remember, rent control can be beaten if the voters understand what it means. Why not do your share to help beat it?

Coming Soon: Soaring Rents

This country is in its worst housing crunch since the 1940s. Whenever a city's vacancy factor sinks below 5 percent, civic authorities start to worry. But the vacancy rate in a lot of cities is now 2 percent and going down, not up.

Shortages could cause rents to double or triple in this decade. In cities with typical rent control ordinances there'll either be urban blight or a black market in rentals, with people paying extra under the table. Within a few years you may see two or three tenants bidding for one unit.

It isn't just *my* opinion that a bad shortage is on the way. The Brookings Institution (a respected, independent research organization in Washington, D.C.) has just published a book, *Rental Housing in the 1980s*. It forecasts a "sharply increased rental cost for many of the nation's estimated 29 million households who are tenants," according to a report on the book in the *Los Angeles Times*. Although Brookings tends to be liberal in its views, it definitely frowns on rent control. Its book states, "The continuation of rental controls only increases the shortage of rental housing and the deterioration of the existing rental inventory."

In California, a prime real-estate market, the rental shortage looms larger month by month. In the 1970s the number of building permits issued each year averaged 212,000. But the average has been only 122,000 a year since 1980. The economists say the only way to bring California's supply of housing abreast of demand would be to build 200,000 units a year for the rest of the decade. In other words, the state is falling farther behind by about 78,000 units every year.

What do these figures tell you? That there is no better time to buy rental housing than now! If you're living in a rented house, brace yourself to see your rent double in a few years. But if you want to keep your housing costs the same, buy a home and establish a payment on its mortgage.

And now, about you owners of rental properties: what will happen to your investments if controls come? Nothing but good, if you own a fourplex, duplex, or single-family home. Units of four and under are exempt from rent control ordinances in most places. The SFH (single-family home) is exempt everywhere, as far as I know.

You can raise your rents on these properties as much as the market will allow, even when your city is under tight rent control. Since a rent rollback or freeze (or even a severe clamp on increases) will create a worse shortage, owners of SFH rentals (and most owners of duplexes and fourplexes) will profit.

Self-Defense for Apartment Owners

But what about bigger rental properties? If you own one, and rent control is being considered in your area, here's something you can do besides campaigning against it.

Say the current month-to-month rent for your apartments is $500. Boost it to $650 on your new rentals but offer a $150-a-month discount. Tell your tenants they get this discount if two things happen:

1. Rent is paid by the third of the month.
2. Rent is paid with a good check.

Two kinds of people will object to your plan: people who pay late and people who write bad checks. Do you want them in your building?

Another benefit of the arrangement: You normally can't evict for nonpayment of late charges. But you *can* evict for nonpayment of rent. The $150 is rent, not late charges.

Now let's follow this idea further. Let's say rent control is voted in. Suppose a year or two passes, and demand in your area warrants a $100 rent raise, or 20 percent. The ordinance says no. But you're still okay. You simply make your discount $50 instead of $150. The rent is still $650 (you haven't raised it) but the tenant pays $100 more. You have raised your income without actually raising the rent.

This method has been tested in court and upheld. You have complied with the ordinance, yet you're collecting 20 percent more rent than you did ($600 instead of $500). With the added benefits of less worry about slow pay and rubber checks, it's a nice package. On top of this, you can still take advantage of whatever rent increases are allowable under the ordinance (usually around 7 or 8 percent per year).

Of course, if rent control is already in force, you can't use this method, and you'd better start looking for ways to dispose of your building. (I'll suggest some in a minute.) Meanwhile you can buy a hundred or more SFHs if you're up to it. Raise their rents as much as the market allows. The Rent Control Board will never bother you. I wouldn't suggest buying duplexes or fourplexes at this time, however. They're not my favorite investments, with or without rent control, because you usually have to pay too much for them, as I explain elsewhere in this book.

To sum up what I've said in the chapter so far: Don't let a rent-control ordinance, or the fear that one will be enacted, keep you from becoming a real-estate investor. There's just too much money to be made.

Now we come to the "worst case" scenario. Maybe by the time you've picked up this book, you already own an apartment building in a city that's under rent control. You're trapped. What should you do?

How to Escape

For one thing, you can buy other apartment buildings —but not in the controlled area. Buy outside it but as close to home as possible, for the reasons I mentioned in Chapter 5. Your properties elsewhere can cushion losses inside the area, and can give you more leeway in working out arrangements to get your equity out of the control zone.

For another thing, start thinking about ways to sell or exchange the building that's controlled. You might think nobody would want to buy it, but you'd be wrong. Take your time and look for a worthwhile way to get it off your hands.

The only apartment owner who gets badly hurt by rent control is one who holds it a long time. For the short term, rent control has little effect on a building's value. The owner can count on his building's staying full. Tenants know that if they move (or if they cause enough trouble to get themselves evicted) their rent will shoot up. Over a long period (fifteen or twenty years) an area under strict rent control will become a slum, as in New York. But for the next few years your property might be a good holding for any owner interested mainly in guaranteed income and a quiet life.

To help him buy, if necessary, review my chapter Twenty-two Ways to Buy if You're Cash Poor (Chapter 8). Turn it around, and suggest some of these ways to the prospective buyer. Sell on soft terms. Nothing down is hard to pass up, especially if the area is fairly nice.

If you aren't comfortable selling for no down payment, you can get protection and still not make your buyer put up cash. Ask him for a blanket mortgage (a mortgage on more than one property). This mortgage would include some other property the buyer owns—his home, apartment building, maybe his car or a vacant lot. Then he has something to lose, even though he put no cash down, because you can foreclose on both properties. After he has paid for several years and is locked in, you might release his other property. This could be part of the original purchase agreement.

When selling seems virtually impossible because every apartment owner in town is trying to sell at sacrifice prices, look farther away. Advertise your building for sale or exchange in big-city newspapers in nearby states. Distant investors (who probably have a saner perspective on the situation than panicky local owners) might be attracted by any of several offers you might advertise.

Solutions by Swapping

For example, you might offer your equity as down payment on a much larger property (three or four times as large). If the owner of the larger property needs to sell, he may consider taking your smaller building as an acceptable nuisance since it gets rid of his building. You might offer cash as a sweetener if you have or can raise some. That is, if he wants a $125,000 down payment you could offer your $100,000 equity in your building plus $25,000 cash.

Another example: a tax-free exchange of your property (plus something else of yours, maybe) for property outside the rent-control area. People will trade for something they wouldn't buy in seven lifetimes. For instance, a person may never even have wished for a motor home, but if you could offer him a motor home for a down payment, he may start to think, "Say I wouldn't mind having a motor home."

Your ads may catch the eye of someone moving to your area who wants to liquidate property where he lives. Probably he'd prefer to sell it, but if you suggest a trade, or offer to take his out-of-state home as a down payment on your apartment building, he might say yes.

Remember, you've got a few years to find the right owner. Keep looking, and you'll move your equity out of the area before you're hurt by the long-term effects of rent control.

20

HOW TO GET
THAT WINNING
FEELING

WELL, YOU'VE ALMOST FINISHED THE BOOK.

Looking for a good place on the shelf to put it? Then you're dead.

The minute this book hits your bookshelf it's all over. The shelf is where you put all the schoolbooks you've never opened since you left school. They are no good to you now.

But if you keep this book with you and use what's in it, you'll find it's different from what you got in school. I'm not criticizing schools and colleges. We couldn't get along without them. They put things in our heads that we need to earn a living—the three Rs, for instance. What they don't teach us is how to become financially independent. Nobody teaches that because they themselves never knew how.

Take Your Choice

Right now, while you're holding this book in your hand and trying to decide what to do with it—while you're deciding, you'll be choosing between the old way of life on the job and a new way of carving out your own piece of the American dream.

Maybe you're a slow decider. Take another minute or two, while we look at some angles of the choice you must make.

Choosing to make a fresh start is terribly hard. It means breaking away from habits of thinking (and doing) that have kept you on a treadmill since you were in school.

Your schools boxed you, packaged you, slid you into a funnel and fed you to corporate America. They taught you that a good job should be your goal in life. When you were small, and then when you were a teenager, you kept hearing, "Work hard in school, because if you get good grades you can get a good job." Sound familiar?

So you got a job. But you can't be quite happy at it, or you never would have picked up this book.

Probably you live among nine-to-fivers who are comfortably stuck in slots, worrying about their pensions. Psychologists call them "other-directed" people. But deep down you may be different, since you've read all the way through this book. Maybe you're one of the rare "self-directed" types. Probably you've tried to climb your corporate ladder without any great success. So now are you ready to look outside?

Understand, there's nothing wrong with a job if you think about it the right way. I'm not advising you to quit just yet. A job is fine *if* you see it as a stepping-stone to something better.

Here's how I hope you think about it: "My job is a temporary inconvenience I'm putting up with for a few more years while I'm building my financial independence."

Do you know what disappears when you start to think like that? Career planning! Your attention shifts away from the organizational rat race, away from keeping your boss happy and catching the eye of higher-ups. Instead you start to focus on your spare-time money-making. You think, "I don't need a better position because I'm not going to be there in three or four years." You still do your best possible work at your job; it's just that your long-term planning changes (a feeling *not* to be shared with your boss).

I've shown you a wide-open, lucrative field. Having read the book, maybe you intend to enter that field. But intentions are worthless by themselves. They're like those New Year's resolutions we joke about. According to the old folk saying, "The road to hell is paved with good intentions," and that's true.

Only one thing will save you financially: Commitment. Doing it. If you put it off you'll never do it.

Chapter 1 sketched the first steps you should take. Have you taken them? Maybe you were waiting to finish the book. But now there's nothing more to wait for. Let's review what you must do.

1. Set goals. Without a goal, you're drifting. Unless your goal is put into words, it isn't definite enough. It's like something far out in the fog. So write it down. The simple act of putting words and numbers on paper will breathe life into your goal.

How about deciding that your goal is buying two properties a year for five years? This will give you ten properties. It will also give you freedom from a boss, freedom from an office, even freedom from the bank.

Make your goal inescapable. Post it on the bathroom wall, paint it on the bottom of your coffee cup, tape it to the inside of your checkbook, do anything you can think of to keep yourself reminded of it.

2. Commit time. That's what it takes to move toward your goal. Set aside five to ten hours per week, as I advised in the beginning. Spend that time hunting for properties, making offers, making purchases.

You'll need willpower. Using that many hours means taking hours away from fun time, travel time, or TV-watching time. Again, if you're a TV addict, take drastic action. Lend it to your mother-in-law. Promise yourself you'll ask for its return when you own two properties, but not until then. In order to watch the playoffs, you'll close on two properties with a speed that will startle you.

3. Get the cheapest five-year diary you can find. Open it every day and log in the hours you spend making

money that day. (Write the zeros very large, so they'll stare at you reproachfully.) Remember, this doesn't mean your job hours. That's just earning a living. We're talking about wealth-building hours.

Keep Score on Yourself

Every Sunday night, add up the time. If it's between five and ten hours (or more) you're on your way. Even if you haven't bought anything yet, you're learning by hunting for buys.

You will find property because you're looking for it. And you will buy property because you're writing offers. There's no other way. No one is going to kick down your door one Sunday while you're watching the National Football League and bring you a building to buy. I missed a lot of football for a few years because I was out buying property, but now I can fly to the Super Bowl and see it in person because I can afford the trip. Pay your dues (mainly time) for a few short years, and you'll live happily ever after.

The diary is your passport, your dues book. If you keep that record faithfully day after week after month after year, you can throw the diary in the trash can, before five years are up, because the need to work forty hours a week at the office will have disappeared from your life. You will then have twenty or thirty hours a week to move around making money, and the rest of the time to enjoy life, because you won't need a job anymore. (As you make your wealth, enjoy it. You can't take it with you, as you've probably heard.)

The goals, the time, and the diary will get you moving. To keep moving, a few additional steps will help immensely. Here they are.

For a Better Marriage

4. Get your spouse actively involved.

I don't think it's a benefit to have both husband and wife involved—I think it's a must!

In the first place, you both have strengths and weaknesses. If your marriage is like most, your weaknesses tend to be your spouse's strengths and vice versa. So you are stronger (and happier) working together. The team is stronger than its parts.

In the second place, wives tend to outlive husbands by an average of about ten years. When a wife becomes a widow, sharks start to gather.

An uninformed, inexperienced widow is easy prey. There is some statistical evidence that, fourteen months after their husbands die, a surprising number of well-to-do widows have used up their insurance money, sold their real estate and their stocks, invested the proceeds foolishly and found themselves destitute.

Care enough to work together with your spouse. Make sure both of you understand the family investments and what they are worth. If your children are old enough and interested enough, get them on the team too.

The Only Way to Buy

5. Write offers. Nothing happens unless you do.

Want to die poor? Read all about real estate, look at a lot of it but don't write offers. Just assume the owners wouldn't sell to you. That's all it takes to fail.

What's a reasonable goal in writing offers? One or two per month, when you're starting. If you're really putting in five or more hours per week (and you won't know unless you record it in your diary) this should not be a problem.

6. Visualize. Make mental pictures.

Your subconscious mind is a powerful weapon. Use

the ten minutes in bed before you fall asleep at night. Get a strong mental image of one thing that you want: boat, car, trip, you pick it. Picture the money spouting up from your properties to pay for this item.

Maybe you'll enjoy visualizing doing something for others—buying your parents that trip they always wanted, or putting them into a nice house, or sending your kids to a great camp.

Visualizing may sound dumb, but it works. Never mind how dumb it sounds—do it! Give it a few weeks to take hold. You'll start waking up with an overwhelming urge to go out and buy property.

Never Stop Learning

7. Take seminars. Best are the intensive short courses.

College extension courses in real-estate investment are mostly theory, unless they're taught by someone who is a successful full-time investor. But seminars are almost always full of down-to-earth knowledge. They're run by people who have gone out and done it. I'll never stop taking them.

They may look expensive, but they're not, because you are trading money for time. Instead of spending years of your life learning by trial and error, you acquire potentially priceless know-how by spending a few days acquiring this knowledge in concentrated form.

8. Read the right books and magazines.

Start to read books on real-estate investing and subscribe to business magazines.

I have never read a book on investing from which I didn't get at least one good money-making idea. If you read twenty books, you'll have twenty new ideas—maybe a hundred. You don't have to buy all the books. Many of them are available through your public library.

As you read, make notes. Whenever you find another

new twist or short-cut or a completely different approach, write it down and keep it handy.

Strength Through Socializing

9. Be a joiner.

I've mentioned your local Apartment Owners' Association. Among other things, it keeps you informed about developments in the city council and the courts and the legislature that may affect your own operations. You can help it work for public policies that help investment.

Get acquainted with individual real-estate investors and chat with them often. It's important for a beginning investor to be around successful people, investors who are already making money in real estate.

Motivational courses? I don't favor them. They can get you fired up, but the effect only seems to last a few days. Worse, they give you an overwhelming urge to ride but don't give you a horse. You run out of the course shouting, "I want to make money!" How? You can't make it without knowledge. You've got to have a vehicle.

On Your Way

Well, that's it.

The door is open to a future bursting with big-money possibilities. The future is now. The only one standing in your way is you.

Keep your agreement with yourself. Keep this book on the night stand where it's always available. Read this chapter several times, and review other chapters whenever a problem arises that they can solve.

Remember, problems are opportunities. Three or four times in your lifetime, a really big opportunity will present itself. When Lady Luck knocks, step out and drag her in. Turn the opportunity into a fortune. I did, and you can too.

Index

About the Author

Hollis Norton, formerly an engineer, was thrown out of his profession in the famous "Class of '69," when hundreds of thousands of aerospace workers were laid off. He worked at odd jobs to support himself for the next few years until he discovered "cashless" investing. Using the methods outlined in this book, and starting "cash poor" and with poor credit, he built wealth for himself and bought millions of dollars' worth of real estate in several states. For over a decade he lectured to thousands of people across the country every year about making the Great American Dream a reality: Start with nothing and build wealth for yourself in a few short years. The author currently resides in Nevada.